DASHA'S JOURNAL

'Dasha is a brilliant feline! She is flat-out funny, wise beyond her cat years and a true champion of autistics everywhere! Read her journal and let her teach you about autism!'

– Liane Holliday Willey, EdD, author of Pretending to be Normal: Living with Asperger's Syndrome

'A heartwarming book providing insights into how autistic persons perceive and interact with the world as only a cat can. As Dasha "meows" about her human members of the family we learn how autism is a different, rather than a disordered way of being. This book is a delightful and informative read.'

– Stephen M. Shore, EdD, Executive Director of Autism Spectrum Disorder Consulting, Board of Directors for the Autism Society of America and the Asperger's Association of New England

'Dasha's Journal is a much needed work that blends the literary journey with an engaging scientific study. The book provides exemplary and cunning analogies to help the reader better appreciate the inner world of the autistic person. The author's thesis exemplifies autism as a different way of thinking with both strengths and weaknesses. The final result is a funny, clever, and up to date exposition of our present day knowledge regarding autism.'

– Manuel F. Casanova, MD, Gottfried and Gisela Kolb Endowed Chair in Psychiatry Associate Chair for Research University of Louisville, KY

'Dasha's Journal is a charming and original way of explaining the mystery that is autism. Dasha is a cat who lives in an "autistic" family. Her observations on the behaviour of both the autistic and neurotypical members of the family put the "problems" of autism into perspective; we are often told that autistic people are "mindblind", but, as Dasha shows, neurotypicals are just as blind to the ways of those who are "differently abled", whether autistics or cats! The Journal is quirky and amusing, but beneath the humour lies a serious and profound examination of autism and the misconceptions that surround it.'

– *Charlotte Moore, author of* George and Sam
and Adults on the Autism Spectrum

'As a person with Asperger's Syndrome, I cannot help but be troubled by how much misinformation abounds concerning autism. However, after reading Dasha's Journal, I have to give T.O. Daria the best objective comment that I can for a non-autistic writer: she gets it absolutely right!'

– *Edgar Schneider, author of* Discovering My Autism: Apologia
Pro Vita Sua (with apologies to Cardinal Newman)

DASHA'S JOURNAL

A Cat Reflects on Life, Catness and Autism

T.O. DARIA

Jessica Kingsley Publishers
London and Philadelphia

First published in 2008
by Jessica Kingsley Publishers
116 Pentonville Road
London N1 9JB, UK
and
400 Market Street, Suite 400
Philadelphia, PA 19106, USA

www.jkp.com

Library of Congress Cataloging in Publication Data
A CIP catalog record for this book is available from the Library of Congress

British Library Cataloguing in Publication Data
A CIP catalogue record for this book is available from the British Library

ISBN 978 1 84310 586 2

Printed and bound in Great Britain by
Athenaeum Press, Gateshead, Tyne and Wear

For My Family

Contents

CHAPTER **1**

My Story
and the Four Reasons
to Write this Book

I love books. Even more than books, I love manuscripts and proofs (these piles of paper that publishers send to the author for proof-reading and indexing). Why do I love them? I like to sleep on them! What can be better than curling up on A4 sheets on the table, feeling the warmth and softness of the paper? The paper that does not make you sink into a hole but holds your body with strength and tenderness at the same time. You wouldn't understand it if you've never experienced it.

Sorry, I forgot to introduce myself. My name is Dasha, and I'm a cat (or feline, to sound more academic). I have a three-bedroom house which I share with several pets of mine: a female with two names – Mother and Wife; a male who is called either Dad or Husband; and two children – a boy Alex (also known as Son and Brother), and a girl Lisa (or Daughter and Sister). Oh, and I have another name as well – Furry Paperweight.

When I arrived into the household, I was very young (just five or six weeks old). I don't remember much about my biological family. My kittenhood was not a very happy one. I was taken from my mother and siblings soon after I was born (just a few weeks old, I guess). My memories of this traumatic event are blurry; the first conscious image of the time is me, living in a cardboard box in a Barnsley pet shop.

> A *pet shop* is a place where humans come to be adopted by the animals who are brave enough to take responsibility for looking after them. Oh, and you can buy food and all the living necessities there, too. Humans don't eat healthy food and their homes lack vital equipment, such as scratching posts or toys to keep your mind and body fit. In a way, animals bring civilisation into the primitive living conditions of their pets. So those fortunate humans who have been adopted suddenly find their lives improving tremendously.

But I digress. Six years ago, on a rainy September afternoon, while I was contemplating my destiny, a Man (who later turned out to be Dad) entered the shop. My box was in the corner, behind the shelves with packets of budgie food. I was deep in thoughts and, at first, didn't pay much attention to the stranger, but soon the man's behaviour made me alert and uncomfortable about his actions. I was not alone in my suspicions. The owner of the shop, while pretending to read a newspaper, was watching the intruder from the corner of his eye. The Man's behaviour was really odd. (Shall I meow 'idiosyncratic'?) The so-called customer scanned the upper shelves with quick short glances across the perimeter of the shop, dancing on his tip-toes. Then he moved to the middle shelves, inspecting each product very carefully. When he reached the section with tinned dog and cat food he tried to look behind them. The owner, though tense, stayed put. The only sign that he was nervous (and undecided whether to call the police right now or wait for a few more minutes) was the trembling newspaper in his left hand. The last straw that made him take action was the stranger's strategy to inspect the lower shelves: he dropped on his fours and attempted to crawl behind the litter boxes. Enough was enough. The owner (literally) sprang into action. He put his right hand on the phone, remembering the location of the keys with 999, and covered the phone with his left hand, still holding the newspaper. This time it was his voice that was trembling as he spoke to the customer.

'C-c-can I help you?'

'I do hope you can.'

And then the trilogue followed.

Trilogue: a conversation between two persons – i.e. a dialogue – ignoring the presence of a third party because: (a) it's a young child who is not supposed to understand what adults are talking about; (b) it's a disabled person who is not supposed to understand what 'normal' people are talking about; (c) it's an animal who is not supposed to understand what humans are talking about. Contrary to this wrong assumption, the third party present – whether (a), (b) or (c) – actually contributes (mentally) to the dialogue, thus creating a trilogue.

The Man put a pleading expression on his face and sheepishly started his unhappy tale.

'I want to buy a kitten, but pet shops do not sell kitties and puppies any more.'

The owner couldn't hide his relief and very quickly restored his authoritative posture.

'Kittens and puppies are not toys! Many parents used to buy them as presents for their children. The novelty didn't last long and with the first puddle on the sofa or the first poo on the carpet, these poor creatures were on the streets – abandoned and miserable. This irresponsibility by many grown-ups is unacceptable!'

'I know! I know! But my family is very responsible, I promise you.'

'Then contact the RSPCA – the charity for protection of animals – and they'll help you to adopt a kitten. [*Adoption?*

Aren't I too young to adopt a family?] You'll find their contact details in the Yellow Pages.'

The Man's face said it all – he lost his last hope.

'We did contact them, and they refused. You see, our house is too close to the main road, and it was assessed as unsafe for a cat. But I can assure you, it's quite safe. Our cat Sally lived in this house for 16 years and nothing happened to her. Sadly, she died last year – of old age. Nothing has been the same ever since. Our family is incomplete. And our home… Without a cat our home is merely a house!'

'*I could consider the proposal.*'

The Man looked around: 'What was that?'

'What was *what?*'

The owner dropped the newspaper at last, but the place to drop it was a bit inappropriate – on my head. '*Outrrrageous!*' The attempt to hide the kitten (who shouldn't have been in the shop, in the first place) failed. Triumphant, the Man picked me up.

'This IS a kitten! Kittens and puppies are not toys! You are not allowed to sell them in the shop…'

The tables were turned. The shop owner tried to win time to think of some plausible explanation. He picked up the newspaper, folded it up and carefully put it on the counter.

'You see,' – he avoided looking at the Man – 'my friend has brought this poor kitten here and asked me to find a good family for her.'

'Well, you've found it. Five pounds.'

The man produced his wallet with his right hand, while holding me against his chest with his left.

'Ten pounds.'

'Deal!'

'*No one has asked ME. I can't adopt your family. I'm under age. To say nothing of the price! Ten pounds – I resent that!*'

To be honest I was quite pleased to have an opportunity to see a larger (than my cardboard box) world. Despite this, I wanted my meow to count – just out of principle!

How did I end up adopting this particular family? The answer is, I liked the house and the garden. The house is big enough to provide space for playing, exercising, having meals and, of course, my favourite activity – sleeping. It took me a couple of months to train my humans. (By the way, among animals, cats are the best behaviour management therapists of humans.) The first three rules I introduced were:

1. I run the house, you pay the bills.

2. Cats always know their rights.

3. All you need to know you can learn from me.

I then worked from there. Now my pets are polite and compliant. They let me choose where I want to sleep (including kitchen towels, children's clothes and furniture). And as for the garden (which is beautiful), it's all mine.

I never thought that I, the Cat, would start writing this journal but four very powerful reasons made me turn to writing (or, to be more exact, turn one of my pets into my secretary by sending my thoughts via the head into the right hand, so that, eventually, they have ended up on paper. If I meowed that I used my own paws to scribble, or what may seem more appropriate to you – but not to me – to type on the computer, you wouldn't believe it, would you? These four reasons are as follows.

My first reason… Well, it's too selfish to state it in the very beginning. I'll disclose it at the end of the book.

Second, the humans I share the house with are obsessed with reading and talking about autism. You see, the Son (aka Brother and Alex) is autistic. Any reasonable 'creature sapiens' would justifiably question this obsession – a member of your family is autistic, now what? Why is it so important to talk about autism non-stop? (I'm a cat, and no one seems to be obsessed with my 'catness' – a unique and fascinating subject, by the way. So I'd like to be even and counterbalance their conversations with my feline perspective.)

Third, from what I've heard many humans compare autistics with cats and non-autistics with dogs. I beg to differ, and I want to show why.

Fourth, THE book was published in 2005 – the book that made the whole household talk about autism and ME (the only representative of the animal kingdom in their isolated world). My life suddenly became intolerable – three of them (Alex was the only one who knew better than to harass the poor defenceless creature) were following me everywhere for hours. Initially (and understandably!), I hated the book and the lady who wrote it, blaming her for turning my housemates into predators of 007 type. After a few days in hiding, however, my curiosity won (without killing me), and I actually started to *listen* to their discussions. The (initially infamous, but eventually my favourite) book is *Animals in Translation: Using the Mysteries of Autism to Decode Animal Behavior*, written by one of the most famous and successful autistics at present – Dr Temple Grandin. She has a special connection with animals because of her autism. It was enough to get me interested in the book, autism and life in general. Could it be that I, Dasha, have a special connection with autistic individuals because of my 'catness'? Dr Grandin says that she sees things about animals that other people don't. Well, I guess I'm in a unique position to see things about autistic and non-autistic people that other creatures don't – I have both species (autistic and non-autistic ones) in my own household. That's how the idea of my own book emerged. I have a perfect laboratory (my house) for my observations and experiments with my unsuspected guinea pigs. Forward!

CHAPTER 2

Disclaimer

My Journal comes out of the six years (in human terms – 40 years)[1] I've spent with Homo sapiens (HSs) of two kinds – autistic and non-autistic ones.

> *Homo sapiens (HS)*: from Latin 'Man Wise' or Wise Man, or human being

It is inspired by Temple Grandin's work with animals. Dr Grandin is one of the very few humans who took the effort to understand (and popularise) the way animals (cats included) experience the world. I'm very grateful for this because thanks to her work other (less perceptive) humans can now appreciate our thinking, emotions, communication, and way of living in general. She says that it is her autism that helps her to interpret animals' behaviours. I want to return the favour and help people to understand autism. How can I do it? It comes with the territory. I'm a cat, aren't I? It's my 'catness' that enables me to 'feel' autism and 'translate' it into English. What I'm trying to meow is, like Temple Grandin, who proves that being autistic makes it easier to understand animals, I, being an animal, will try to make it easier to understand autism.

This Journal is my humble attempt to enable non-autistic HSs to appreciate autistic abilities that are so different from 'normal' functioning, while revealing the myths and untrue speculations about animals, cats in particular. Unlike Temple Grandin, I haven't published hundreds of scientific papers, and this is my first research study. So, please bear this in mind and don't be too harsh with me – I'm still learning.

I can hear all the outrage about my endeavour to write a book. Doesn't everyone agree that anthropomorphising animals isn't a good idea? And you know what? I'm absolutely certain that it's still important to *think* from the animal's point of view in order to imagine at least what is going on in their minds. Though animals are *not* four-legged humans, they still have their own intellectual, emotional and social lives. The best thing any writer who takes up the challenge of understanding animals can do is to make a good guess. My Journal is as good an attempt to give some information about autism and animals as any other book. Look at it as just another way to discuss very important subjects. Take it or leave it. Full stop. Oh, if you want to argue or refute my stance, talk to the paw! (Just kidding.)

CHAPTER 3

What is Autism?
That's the Question

So, the first question to answer is – What is autism? Do you want good or bad news first? (As a rule, HSs ask for bad news first, but we know better, don't we?) The good news is that thousands of researchers around the world are looking for the answer. The bad news is that nobody seems to have found it yet. I, for one, am not satisfied with the official definition of autism as a lifelong developmental disability that typically appears during the first three years of life, and affects the way the person functions in three areas – known as the Triad of Impairments – social interaction, communication, and rigidity of thought and behaviours.[1] Don't you smell a rat here? You cannot see these impairments in newborns. The child has to be at least 12 to 16 months old to display difficulties in social interaction and communication. Surely there must be something else involved in the earlier stages of their development, maybe even during their mother's pregnancy. The problem is that this 'something' is not visible to humans (they are blind, deaf and dumb, in comparison with us animals anyway!), so professionals have opted for the 'surface behaviours' and introduced the Triad of Impairments. As a result, we have all ended up in a mess. On the one paw, the Triad is good to recognise (and diagnose) autism; on the other paw, it has brought all sorts of misconceptions, misunderstanding and frustrations for all the parties involved.

Let me give you a couple of examples to illustrate my point. A person with Condition 'A' enters a room and goes along its perimeter, touching the walls and pieces of furniture on his way. Someone offers him a plate with biscuits and a cup of tea. He ignores the biscuits and knocks down the tea with his hand. Eventually he settles down in the armchair in the corner of the room, looking in the opposite direction from the host and other humans present. When he starts talking he appears to address his request for a cup of tea to the fireplace, forgetting to apologise for the broken cup and the spoilt carpet. Or consider another situation. A person with Condition 'B' looks out of the window while you are talking to him. The person ignores you completely. Do these individuals seem to have social and communication impairments? Absolutely (with the emphasis on 'seem')! Do they need help? Of course they do. But if the main focus were on the development of social and communication skills, the outcome would be disastrous. However, if we identified the conditions correctly ('A' as blindness, and 'B' as deafness) we could explain the person's social and communication 'impairments' as consequences of his inability to see or to hear, and the programmes to help them would be different. In both cases, the trick is to understand what the problem is, adjust the environment and find ways to communicate with 'socially and communicatively impaired' individuals. Their conditions would suddenly become less disabling.

To complicate matters even further, authorities in the field of autism have introduced another term – Autism Spectrum Disorders (ASDs) – that, like an umbrella, covers a number of conditions resulting in the Triad of Impairments. The most interesting (and controversial) condition among ASDs is Asperger syndrome. Some researchers consider it as a higher-functioning autism, while others insist on its separateness from autism. Yet no one knows the right answer!

As autism is a spectrum disorder, some individuals may be severely affected, while for others their difficulties may appear to be subtle. A very distinguished psychiatrist, Lorna Wing,[1] who introduced the Triad of Impairments, gives examples of different degrees of severity of social interaction deficits. They range from complete 'aloofness' (when children seem to live in their own world), via 'passive' states (when persons respond to social approaches but do not initiate them), to 'active but odd' ways of interaction (when individuals do want to interact but fail to follow social rules of accepted social contact), to 'stilted' or 'formal' social interaction (when a person's manner of interacting is deemed inappropriate at worst, or eccentric at best, because he or she is too formal and rigid). What baffles me completely is that it is the *way* autistic individuals interact that is described as 'impaired'. Why, I wonder? The subject of my research – Alex – interacts with his family, and even strangers, all the time, whether in his 'passive' or 'active but odd' way. Why is he '*impaired* in social interaction'? Just because the majority of HSs find his approaches strange and bizarre? Poor boy. He's had many a time when it was he who was puzzled by people's reactions! For example, last Saturday the whole family went for a walk (with me crawling after them from bush to bush – I take my research responsibilities very seriously). Turning to the field from our footpath (when I thought my experiment would end as there were no trees or bushes around), the family bumped into an old lady walking her dog. Luck was with me – the main part of my research test unfolded right there.

This is the transcript of what followed, interspersed with my research notes. Alex (having learned his 'social interaction lessons' of being polite) approached the lady, pointed his

```
when awake I'll analyse the situations I've
passively observed, draw conclusions and put
forward hypotheses.
```

What worries me about this second ('communication') aspect of the Triad is the assumption that autistic individuals do not communicate (or don't want to communicate). I beg your pardon, but it's just not true. I can assure you that they *do* communicate. It's HS blindness that prevents the non-autistic HSs from seeing their attempts to converse. That is why many autistic children stop trying to get their messages across. Of course, if it is something important (I'd meow, vital) they want to communicate (for instance, 'I'm in pain. Help me,' or 'I've had enough. Leave me alone!') to the non-autistic HSs (who know only their own language and expect the whole world to speak it), they have to make these HSs listen. And you know what? The non-autistic humans interpret (or should I meow 'misinterpret'?) their messages as 'challenging behaviours' and do their best to shut the desperate child up, without providing any other tool for communication, or learning their child's special language (that I'll investigate a bit later).

The same has happened in the world of animals. I'm not pulling your hind leg, and I don't want to meow the obvious (I do apologise to those who have never doubted it) but all animals (cats included) can talk and communicate. And purrleeease, don't simplify our language to 'meowing'. If the humans can't interpret it, it's their problem, not mine. For example, my 'meowewou' ('I want my food, preferably tuna) is completely different from 'miaowouiew' ('Open the door! I have to go outside. NOW!'). Mind you, my patience with the 'illiterate lot' is admirable. I always check whether they've got my message, and I'm quite happy to repeat it again and again (and again, if necessary) to help them comprehend it. The problem arises when it is urgent and they can't work it out. Is it my fault that I can't hold it any longer and deliver the contents of my bowels or bladder onto the carpet? Instead of complaining about my 'toileting problems', they'd be better learning my communication system. Why is it always one-sided? I, for one, have learned 'humanese' – at least, the one that is spoken by the four pets of mine. What is more, I'm quite fluent in understanding their non-verbal communication. I know when they are happy or unhappy, angry or relaxed, by the tone of their voice and body movements. I confess I have problems with reading their facial expressions. But it's not because I'm unable to do it; I just don't like to look at their bald faces. I bet some HSs do not believe that I, like other animals, can communicate not only my needs but also my feelings and attitudes. Those who live with us learn pretty soon. For example, when Dad took me to the vet last month (with a very poor excuse that I needed a jab to protect me from the cat flu), I expressed my feelings as soon as we got home – I peed under his favourite armchair! Isn't it a clever way to deliver my smelly message? I hope he had enough time to 'read' and comprehend it while wiping it from the floor. By his reaction (swearing) I knew he interpreted it correctly – I wished him to experience the needle in *his* backside!

The third part of the Triad is even more confusing than the previous two. In the past, it was labelled as 'impairments in imagination'. Then the experts changed it to 'rigidity of thought and behaviours'. These include an inability to play imaginatively with objects or toys, or with other children, stereotyped activities and rigidity of thinking patterns. If autistics are impaired in imagination, does it mean that those who have expressed their creativity in writing, art, science and other spheres, are not autistic?

There are many other misconceptions created by the official definition. For example, 'autistic people lack empathy and/or emotions'. As always, researchers have provided theoretical foundations for this unjustified assumption. The best known is the Theory of Mind that is (allegedly) absent in autism. According to this Theory, autistic people have difficulty in understanding other people's feelings, emotions and behaviours. In short, they cannot 'try someone else's shoes on'. (Did I get it right? I find it difficult to remember idioms that are irrelevant to me. I don't wear shoes, or any other useless things on my body, for that matter.)

> *Idioms*: groups of words that do not mean what they really mean. You have to look behind the literal meaning and learn the hidden message of each expression. Non-autistic HSs invented idioms in order to confuse autistic people.

To make it easier to understand what 'lack of Theory of Mind in autism' means, I'll translate it into proper English: Can you get under my skin? Can you wear my fur? (or my 'fur coat' – for non-autistic HSs who seem to lack literal understanding of words and always prefer to disguise them with other words). Of course, you can't. It means you lack Theory of my Mind because you don't know what my fur feels like on my body. (If you want to check your ability to understand my Theory of Mind, there is a short test in Box 3.1.)

So what is this fuss about? We all 'lack Theories of Others' Minds'. Some non-autistic HSs wouldn't agree with my arguments. They think that *all* creatures should feel the same about different experiences and events. It leaves Alex and me in a minority. For example, while the majority enjoy fireworks, I accompany Alex under the bed, waiting for the torture to be over. Another ill-effect of the Theory of Mind is that some researchers believe it is only about autism and forget that other disorders may be characterised by lack of this Theory. Thus, my (not favourite) neighbour – a black cat called by her servants (humans sharing the house with her)

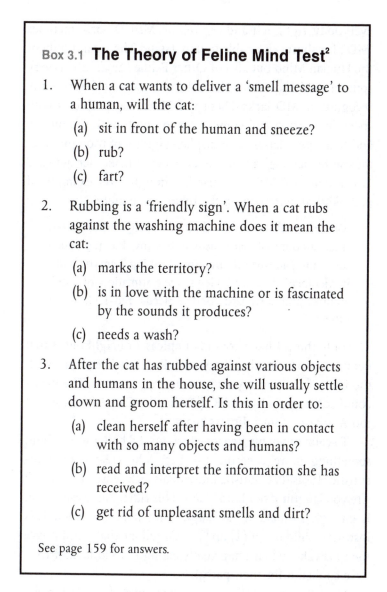

Box 3.1 **The Theory of Feline Mind Test[2]**

1. When a cat wants to deliver a 'smell message' to a human, will the cat:

    (a) sit in front of the human and sneeze?

    (b) rub?

    (c) fart?

2. Rubbing is a 'friendly sign'. When a cat rubs against the washing machine does it mean the cat:

    (a) marks the territory?

    (b) is in love with the machine or is fascinated by the sounds it produces?

    (c) needs a wash?

3. After the cat has rubbed against various objects and humans in the house, she will usually settle down and groom herself. Is this in order to:

    (a) clean herself after having been in contact with so many objects and humans?

    (b) read and interpret the information she has received?

    (c) get rid of unpleasant smells and dirt?

See page 159 for answers.

Most Delightful, by herself Me, the Divine, and by all the cats, dogs and pigeons in the neighbourhood Mouth that's Dirty (because she is so full of herself and criticises everything and everybody, right, left and centre), or 'MtheD', or sometimes 'MD', for short – is unable to understand Theory not only of the Human Mind but also of Other Feline Minds. She is very spiteful and believes that she is the only cat who deserves any recognition. MD lacks Theory of Mind, has problems with social interaction and communication with both the human and feline population, and displays rigidity of thought ('me-me-me-meoawing' all the time). Does it make her autistic? Oh, kitten, no! MD is a classic (though rare) example of pathological narcissism in the feline community.

> *Narcissism*: self-love, self-admiration, self-centredness. A small amount of narcissism is healthy, but too much turns into *pathological narcissism*, thinking 'I am the best', intolerance of others' views, overestimation of one's abilities and disregard for the needs and feelings of others.

The only thing I like about my unpleasant neighbour is that her name can be nicely abbreviated. Recently I've played with the idea of making my name sound mysterious. The best I could come up with was DC (Dasha, the Cat). Does it sound too American? But I digress again.

To calm down my negative feelings, I'd better write about something more cheerful: the best joke created by non-autistic HSs is that 'autistic individuals lack sense of humour'! Are you laughing out loud? I am. This ridiculous assumption is enough to make a cat laugh! Isn't it funny, when HSs instruct a child to 'sit (↓) up (↑)'? Or tell me that I 'can't have the tuna cake' when I'm actually eating it. (Bad luck, if they have cooked it for their party.)

Do you think that I'm now going to purr about autism as a misunderstood and mistreated condition? Do you think I'll join a small army of politically correct 'we-autistics' who fight for the rights to be considered superior HSs in no need of treatment? Right? Wrong! If you anticipated this fashionable stance from me, you've failed to imagine what it is like to wear my fur (i.e. you lack my Theory of Mind). Yes, I'm the first to help HSs understand features of autistic functioning and celebrate many amazing abilities they possess. But I'm the last to deny that autism may be VERY disabling. My three pets are still recovering from the shock after Alex hospitalised the entire swimming-pool staff (four with concussions and two with dislocated limbs). Our kind and gentle boy can have his difficult moments when he is not in control of his behaviours because of his autism. He suffers from his 'panic attacks' as much as the person(s) who happens to be at the receiving end. I don't agree with the explanation provided by the politically correct 'we-autistics' that these attacks, as well as digestive problems and sensory processing difficulties, are co-morbid conditions that have nothing to do with autism.

> *Co-morbid condition*: in plain English this is a condition/disorder that co-occurs with any other condition. In an 'autism-is-beautiful' interpretation, a co-morbid disorder is anything negative about autism.

If you want to play these 'autistic-rights-to-be-what-they-are-no-matter-what' games, talk to one (or both) of my hind paws! I try to be objective and get to the root of the problem. (Personally, I would agree with the statement that cats are superior to humans, but for the sake of objectivity, I wouldn't insist on it.) So far, my conclusion is that autism (like any other condition, including 'non-autism') may have both abilities and deficits. And what is more, autism (like non-autism) can co-occur with other psychiatric disorders, for example schizophrenia, personality disorders, psychotic and mood disorders.[3] Though this view is unpopular, someone has to be brave enough to state it loud and clear. (I am *very* independent in my thinking. A cat may look at a king, you know.)

So, what is autism? Is it a combination of impairments in social interaction, communication and imagination? Is it lack of Theory of Mind? A different sense of humour? Is it a disability or a condition? There are more questions than answers. If we don't know what autism is, there are even more problems finding its causes. In fact, several different causes may lead to the same Triad of behaviours known as autism. Maybe there are different 'autisms'?

At present, no single theory accounts for all manifestations of this condition. And no single treatment works for all autistic individuals. However, I urge all HSs involved to be optimistic (you haven't got nine lives to solve this puzzle). Together we can shed some light on this situation. Brain research shows some structural and functional differences between autistic and non-autistic brains that could be a starting point for a real exploration of autism. (One of the researchers has a very famous – but in quite a different field – name. I don't remember it right now. Shakespeare? Travolta? Prescott? No. I have to check all the data before I put it on paper – I do take my research responsibilities seriously.)

Having dealt with the misconceptions of autism, I'll move onto a more personal domain – misconceptions about animals. I apologise beforehand for any emotional outbursts you encounter in the next section, but sometimes when HSs talk (rubbish) about animals, it feels as if someone is rubbing my fur the wrong way!

CHAPTER **4**

Animals and Humans, Cats and Dogs... What are You Trying to Meow?

There are as many misconceptions concerning animals (cats in particular) as there are misinterpretations of autism. Here I'll try to put the facts right and dismantle the stereotypes (created by HSs, of course). Let's deal with the commonest comparisons: cats and dogs (this part is VERY personal), and animals and humans (both sapiens and not-very-sapiens – I mean, some politicians and other individuals who are obsessed with their self-importance).

Cats and dogs

A typical stereotype (and a very fashionable one at present) is to compare autistic humans with cats and non-autistics with dogs. Some stretch the analogy even further and say that having autism is like being a cat in a world of dogs. It's a joke, really. (Sometimes I wonder whether HSs are able to use their brains at all. Why can't they see the obvious and manage to see something that doesn't exist?) And to be fair, why is it considered to be wrong to anthropomorphise animals, but it seems OK to animalise humans; in this case, to felinise autistics and caninise non-autistics? Could you leave us alone, please?

Anthropomorphism: the attribution of human behaviour or personality to non-human animals.

'*Felinism*': the attribution of cat behaviour or personality to non-feline (usually human) animals. You wish!

'*Caninism*': the attribution of dog behaviour or personality to non-canine (usually human) animals.

With all my respect for Donna Williams (and I have a huge respect for this courageous autistic woman who has done so much to help both non-autistics and autistics understand the condition), I absolutely disagree with her analogy of 'cat people' (autistics) and 'dog people' (non-autistics). (To rephrase Socrates' famous statement, Donna 'is a friend but truth is yet a greater friend'.[1]) Just because cats are more independent than dogs does not make them look like autistics. Quite the contrary is true. How many autistic humans (especially those at the lower end of the spectrum) can live independently? Cats are said to dislike new experiences and to avoid strangers. But what about cats' curiosity? It doesn't go together with avoidance of new experiences, does it? (Cats are both very cautious and curious at the same time.) But let us make a proper analysis of this fashionable misconception.

I've read somewhere that unlike dogs, which live in packs and are very social animals, my close relatives (wild, non-domesticated cats) are solitary creatures. What rubbish! To say something like this is an (unsuccessful and ill-informed) attempt to stereotype 'catness'. In fact, not all dogs are 'social creatures' and not all cats avoid humans and other animals. Cats are much more social than many humans realise; sister cats even help each other give birth.[2] Some domesticated felines (and my predecessor, Sally, is a very good example) love human contact and seek attention from their humans all the time they are awake. Sally used to demand 'social and tactile' stimulation. She would approach anyone (a member of her household or a visitor), stuff her head under the hand of her human communicative partner and push the hand, indicating she wanted to be stroked. If her social partner didn't respond appropriately (was impaired in social communication?) the clever feline was only too happy to repair their 'conversation' herself. She would arch her back, push her whole body forward and move under the hand as if it were a piece of furniture, thus successfully giving herself a pat on the back. Sally is not an exception. Far from it! She is a representative of a huge group of domesticated feline creatures who are very people-oriented with a broad repertoire of social interaction strategies they use with 'socially impaired' or 'communicatively retarded' HSs. The most common strategies are: attaching themselves to an individual HS as soon as the person enters the house, following the person wherever he goes, jumping on the lap if he is careless enough to sit down, and then producing vocal utterances expressing either pleasure (when the HS strokes the cat) or fury (when he tries to disturb the creature).

If certain HSs want a better emphasis on 'unsociability', why do they want to use 'cat metaphors'?

> *Metaphor* is a descriptive word or phrase that is applied to an object or an action, even if it has nothing to do with it! To understand metaphors you have to forget about literal meanings of words and use your imagination. For example, 'cat-eyed' or 'cat eye' doesn't mean 'somebody with cat eyes', but rather 'somebody able to see in the dark'.

Why don't they compare autistics with *seemingly* more unsocial animals than cats, for example, giraffes? At least, it would be more logical. Giraffes do *appear* uninterested in the company of others. But, no. Everybody wants to be a cat. Of course, I don't blame them – cats are beautiful and intelligent creatures. However, for the sake of precision, giraffes are a much better comparison. Even the fact that HSs used to think that giraffes do not form relationships and friendships, because their attachments are expressed differently from the way humans expect them, is similar to the misinterpretation of 'autistic social impairments'. Just because giraffes do not run around each other and do not wave their tails when humans are approaching does not mean they are 'socially impaired'. Wrong assumptions again.

Dogs are said to show their feelings openly, while cats keep their own council. I beg to disagree. For instance, if I am not happy with my housemates, they will know my feelings, I can assure you.

The 'cats and dogs' analogy is extremely inaccurate. Cats function the way they are supposed to function. And dogs are perfectly 'doggy' in their behaviour. Their neurology in each case is their normal feline and canine neurology. However, there may be cases when some cats and dogs have neurological problems or have different neurology and they can be seen as having autism, attention deficit hyperactivity disorder (ADHD), depression, mood disorders and so on. This is true of any animal. For example, prematurely separating an elephant from the family tribe, and lack of parental love could leave the animal with severe psychological problems and behavioural difficulties, including aggression.[3] Dawn Prince-Hughes writes about one possible case of autism in a wild chimpanzee, with clear 'symptoms' of perseverative behaviour, poor impulse control, aggression, lack of social skills and poor tolerance of change.[4] He was very dependent on his mother for many years past the age when other young chimpanzees become autonomous.

Animals and humans

It's funny, really, that HSs have been obsessed with aliens and alien intelligence for centuries, while ignoring the intelligence that is here, on this planet – the animal intelligence. If you think about it, humans misunderstand and misjudge animals as beings on a much lower level of development than themselves. Let us start with the obvious – we are *all* animals: 'human animals' and 'non-human animals', or Human (or Homo) sapiens (HSs) and non-Human sapiens (nHSs). (HSs seem to think they are gods in relation to nHSs, and anybody whose image is different from theirs is inferior. Fortunately, we cats are on this earth to remind humans they are not divine and can be treated as *our* servants!) We, nHSs and HSs, have a lot of differences, that's for sure, but to assume that 'non-human animals' are inferior to 'human animals' is a sign of ignorance and arrogance. Just because humans do not know (and cannot imagine) animals' abilities, and always judge them by human standards does not mean we are of lower intelligence. HSs are blind to what we can see, deaf to what we can hear, to say nothing about their inability to smell and taste. (I know, I'm repeating myself, but it's true.)

To make it easier for human animals to understand that non-human animals are intelligent, conscious, rational and feeling non-human beings, I'll start with apes, who resemble humans in their physical appearance. It will help HSs to focus their attention on the subject of the discussion. Recent research has revealed startling similarities in the structure of DNA in apes and humans. Genetically the difference is very small. Anatomically, the chimpanzee brain is the same as the human brain, only smaller.[5] The leading primatologist, Jane Goodall, who worked with chimpanzees in Africa for several decades, observed in chimpanzees many characteristics that were thought to be unique to humans. Animals feel a range of emotions: joy, sorrow, despair (both mental and physical), suffering (both mental and physical), compassion and love; they demonstrate many intellectual skills that were believed to be unique to humans.[6] Sceptics would argue that apes cannot talk (the possession of language, they think, is a unique human characteristic). Some HSs just cannot grasp the idea that animals talk because their language does not resemble human speech. In fact, to equate communicative ability to gestural or vocal responses is anthropocentric.[7] The inability of some HSs to understand that 'language' (as a tool of communication and thinking) is not necessarily a verbal one, is breathtaking. Researchers at St Andrew's University have found that animals not only talk in 'words' but also in 'sentences'.[8] Using a series of sounds, they are able to communicate such complex ideas as, for example, 'There's a nasty leopard over there. Let's go somewhere safer.' If humans hear only 'agrhmeekklous' and think it's meaningless, whose intelligence is doubtful in this case?

What is more, those animals who have been in contact with humans can learn to understand 'humanese' as well. For example, apes know that a word can refer to a 'thing'; they can distinguish between the colours and even use numerals; they can follow complex spoken requests such as, for example, 'Get the noodles that are in the bedroom.' In one laboratory, apes were reported to understand more than 3000 words.[9] Koko, a lowland gorilla, learned more than 1000 words of American Sign Language from Dr Penny Patterson, a researcher at Stanford University.[10] (How many humans can understand animals' languages? OK, a simpler one: How many humans know foreign languages? For Koko and many other nHSs, sign and verbal humanese are foreign languages.) Of course, when this case study was reported in the media, some sceptics (not very sapient humans) denied her this ability and interpreted the results as learning the tricks to get rewards. But Koko proved her linguistic abilities by coming up with neologisms and phrases where she substituted the words she didn't know with words from her vocabulary.

Neologism: a new word or expression created to name something that has not yet the definition in one's vocabulary.

For example, she would sign 'eye hat' for a mask, 'finger bracelet' for a ring, and 'lettuce hair' for parsley.[11] (Aren't human toddlers going through the same stage while acquiring their language?) Koko not only communicated in a foreign language but was also very patient with her human communicative partners when she wanted to get her message across. For example, to describe brussels sprouts (not a word to start learning a foreign language with) Koko signed 'little stink balls' (I absolutely agree with her description of this disgusting food. Humans should include it as a dictionary definition for this vegetable.) Koko's IQ measured on the Standford Binet Intelligence Test was 85, and on the Peabody Picture Vocabulary Test was 81.6. (Mind you, they used IQ tests designed for *human animals*, not specifically for *non-human animals*.) If HSs measure their human abilities by the non-human IQ tests, where will they find themselves – on the borderline? in the region of mild or severe mental retardation? If you want to experience unfairness of IQ tests for yourself and get the idea what it is like to be doomed as an idiot, try to do the nHS IQ test (Box 4.1).

Of course, some may try to refute animal intelligence with the 'Clever Hans story'. (It's impossible to discuss intelligence of animals without mentioning Clever Hans.) However, this story confirms the fact that animals are intelligent, but their abilities are so different that some HSs fail to see them. From the very beginning, the humans misinterpreted Hans' phenomenon. Let us look at it from the perspective of different abilities:

Box 4.1 **The nHS IQ test**[12]

1. Can you identify the position of a distant object (e.g. 2–3 miles away from you) in relation to the direction of the sun and communicate its location, distance and desirability to your friend via a waggle dance?

    Yes: 5

    No: 0

2. Can you see ultraviolet?

    Yes: 5

    No: 0

3. In a dark unfamiliar room can you identify the objects under the table?

    Yes: 5

    No: 0

4. Using *seismic communication* (making the ground rumble by stomping on it), can you send a message to your friend who lives 20 miles away from you?

    Yes: 5

    No: 0

5. Can you memorise a 9000-mile route across unmarked open terrain after travelling just once?

    Yes: 5

    No: 0

6. Take 500 nuts and bury them one by one in 500 holes in a park. How many nuts can you recover

after two months (using the method of triangulation, relying on the relative position of trees and buildings, and the angles and distances between these distant landmarks)?

1–10:   1

11–100:   2

101–200: 3

201–400: 4

401–500: 5

7. Can you predict a seizure in a person 30 minutes before it happens?

Yes: 5

No: 0

Now add your points together and check the nHS IQ:

0–10: severe mental retardation

11–20: borderline

21–30: average abilities

31–35: higher than average

Are you happy with the results? That's exactly how we, animals, feel when humans treat us as 'mindless creatures' who have only reflexes and instincts, and are in need of 'behaviour training'.

In the beginning of the twentieth century, a retired German mathematics teacher discovered what he thought to be amazing capabilities and human-like intelligence in his horse

Hans. Hans seemed to know many facts from different disciplines and could answer questions (by tapping his foot an appropriate number of times to indicate the right answer). The whole scientific (and not very scientific) community mobilised their intellectual powers to prove that Hans was NOT intelligent, and that there was something else in place. (Why can't humans be happy about animals being clever? It would mean they wouldn't look at animals as their inferiors but just as different species that should be respected for what they are. Is it too much for a human being to take in?) Eventually a psychologist, Oscar Pfungst, discovered that Hans was unable to answer the question if the questioner did not know the right answer, or if the person asking the question stood behind the screen and Hans could not see him. It turned out that Clever Hans was using subtle visual cues (unconscious body language and facial expressions) to get his answers right. Pfungst thought he found the explanation and Hans was not clever after all. A very human explanation! Why did nobody admire Hans' intelligence to 'read' humans and communicate with them? Isn't it a sign of a very high intelligence? Can humans 'read' animals or even their own species with the accuracy Clever Hans displayed? Try, for example, to guess what I was thinking about when the picture on the next page was being taken. So who is clever?

And don't forget about the animals who, some suggest, may be more intelligent than humans – dolphins. Their sonar systems are not very well understood by HSs, but at least researchers do not dispute their ability to communicate and comprehend the world around them. The research on wild bottleneck dolphins has shown that they are among the animals' quickest learners of new sounds, have the ability to recognise themselves and other members of their society as individuals with separate identities and personalities, and even have their own names – 'signature whistles'.[13] The

What is Dasha thinking about?

researchers discovered that dolphins responded to the whistles of their relatives and mates while ignoring those whom they didn't know.

The best illustration of how hopeless HSs are in their ability (inability?) to understand nHSs is their misleading choice of words, for example, 'birdbrain'.

> *Birdbrain*: a derogatory term used by HSs to mean 'a stupid person'. In fact, their inability to grasp the intelligence of birds makes them look mentally retarded themselves.

For centuries HSs (slow learners) have assumed that birds cannot really talk though some of them can imitate human speech without any understanding of what they are 'saying'. Humans like to teach their feathery pets to repeat silly phrases for their own amusement. But an African grey parrot, Alex, proved them all wrong. Dr Irene Pepperburg (not all humans are hopeless) taught the parrot basic English. He not only vocalised phrases and sentences, he knew what he was talking about. He understood such concepts as shape, colour and texture. Like Koko, he invented words to describe objects for which he hadn't been taught names. For instance, he described 'apple' as 'bannery' (combining two words he knew – 'banana' and 'cherry').[14]

Researchers have also discovered that chimpanzees can recognise themselves in mirrors.[9] The 'mirror test' was invented by a scientist called Gordon Gallup in 1970. It has been used many times on different species. The mirror is placed in front of the animal, and if the animal shows that it recognises its own reflection (by touching the spot painted on the forehead, for example, while ignoring another invisible mark on the head, which shows that the animal is not reacting to touch or smell), it's clear that the animal knows who stares at it from the looking-glass. The researchers believe that those who can pass this test possess true 'self-awareness', i.e. a conscious feeling of self as separate from the world. Are you ready by now, if I introduce other animals as self-aware creatures with full mental, emotional and social lives, even if their physical appearance is different from that of humans? So far, apart from apes, the animals who have passed the test are elephants, dolphins and... pigeons. By the way, human cubs (sorry, children) under the age of about 18 to 20 months often cannot do it!

Many animals are fascinated by mirrors but, the researchers claim, they do not seem to realise that what they see is their own reflection. Dogs and cats usually fail this test. But what does it prove? Do the scientists want to meow that felines, canines and some other animals are 'less aware of themselves' and 'not properly conscious'? Has anyone thought about the inappropriateness of this test? Has anyone doubted that the tests invented by humans for humans may be misleading when used with non-human animals? Take, for example, such humble animals as sheep. The researchers who have been studying these creatures (and thank Bast and Sekhmet, who haven't used the misleading 'mirror test') discovered that sheep have very good memories and can recognise each other's voices and at least 50 faces (both of humans and their relatives and mates). Besides, sheep, unlike humans, eat healthy food and if they have health problems (for instance, heartburn or constipation) these bright nHSs know what to eat to ease their discomfort.[15] (Can all humans prescribe their own medication?)

> *Bast and Sekhmet*: two Egyptian 'feline Goddesses'. Bast is the Goddess of Lower Egypt and protector of cats, women and children. Typically she is depicted as a young woman with the head of a cat. Another popular depiction of Bast is her earthly form, as a seated cat. (When in this form her name changes to Bastet.) Sekhmet is the Goddess of Upper Egypt, depicted as a woman with the head of a lioness.

Some animals may not recognise themselves in the mirror not because they lack self-awareness but because their visual perception is different. Their eyes see shadows and movements, and identify them in the mirror just the way they really look – shadows and movements. Just because some animals see what is really there does not mean they are less intelligent. They may be self-aware through other senses (for example, hearing, smell or body awareness).[16] The mirror test fails to identify modality-specific senses of self-awareness among animals. It is another reason why I find it easy to sympathise with autistic humans; for many years their intelligence has been measured with IQ tests that are designed to measure the intelligence of non-autistics. The abilities of autistics, while 'invisible', are so unusual that no existing test can measure them. As autistic individuals have different information processing strategies and styles, they might struggle with tasks presented in a conventional non-autistic way. It is the same as the researchers testing the IQ of a blind person by asking him to name the colours of the objects he was given. Even using his hands he would not be able to pass the test successfully. Does it mean that he would be diagnosed as intellectually deficient? (I'll return to this later.)

Where was I? Oh, yes, 'non-human animals' and their 'human abilities'. Many humans can use tools, and some humans can make them. Many animals can make tools and many animals can use them. So where do you see 'superiority'? For example, apes can use sticks to fish for insects (and they are not taught by humans how to do it). Some birds (wrongly characterised by humans as 'birdbrains') can make tools: crows are skilful at making hooks from pieces of wire, and even use cars (driven by humans) to crack nuts for them by dropping nuts on busy roads. Whether some animals fail the mirror test or pass it, we all have minds and mental lives. If humans cannot figure it out, whose problem is it?

Even ants, these tiny insects with tiny brains, are more 'human' than HSs can imagine (imagination impairments?). In fact, ants are among the most extraordinary animals in the world. They are social insects that live in structurally and socially organised colonies. Ant behaviour is very sophisticated: they have a very complex communication system and social hierarchy and highly developed organisational skills. Recent research has revealed that ants are engaged in 'teaching' their youngsters – not just 'showing' what and how to do, but actively instructing their 'students', with the 'teacher-ant' sharing the knowledge with others without any benefit to the teacher. If we add ants' 'caring' skills, the tiny insects deserve all the respect they can get. For example, ants are the only nHSs known to 'farm' other animals. They nurture their 'cattle' (caterpillars and aphids), keep them safe and comfortable for the food (sugary secretion) they produce. The comparison between the care provided by ants to their 'farm animals' and HSs' historical 'master–slave' relationship is not in favour of the humans.[17]

So far we have dealt with similarities between HSs and nHSs. Of course, there are differences as well. Before we proceed any further, I'd like to emphasise a very important point: every creature (both human and non-human) has senses/cognition/intelligence for their own particular world. They have developed abilities necessary for their needs in their environment. (That's why the results of laboratory experiments should be interpreted with caution; they are not necessarily valid because animals in their natural habitat behave differently from those in artificial environments.) Place a human animal into the natural environment of an elephant, for example, and then compare the IQs – who will look like an idiot? I don't want to give you the right answer but I can tell you, it won't be the elephant! The level of development cannot be described in terms of 'low/high' or 'superior/inferior' as it is tuned to the necessities of each particular species.

Another thing we have to discuss is the brain, one of the most important organs of thinking, feeling and perceiving. However, recent research has revealed that organs other than the brain may carry 'memory' and 'emotional reactions' to things, people and events. Some intriguing revelations of those with organ-transplants make one doubt whether the brain is the only organ that matters in 'meaningful functioning'. Professor Gary Schwartz suggests this phenomenon can be explained by 'cellular memory', when cells other than brain cells are involved in learning and memory.[18] Concerning the brain, however, there are two issues to consider: size and complexity of structure.

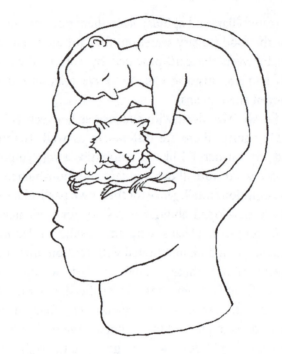

Three brains in one (drawing by Ian Wilson)

Temple Grandin devoted a section of her book to explaining the evolution, similarities and differences between the brains of animals and humans. She named the section 'Lizard Brains, Dog Brains, and People Brains'. (I'd prefer to change 'dog brains' into 'cat brains' in the title, but, well, I'm biased…) Dr Grandin describes a 'three-brain theory' ('triune brain theory') introduced by Paul MacLean.[19] According to this theory, the human brain is arguably 'three different brains each one built on top of the previous at three different times in evolutionary history':

1. The 'oldest' brain is the 'reptilian brain', responsible for basic life support functions, for example, breathing. It corresponds to that in lizards.

2. The 'middle' brain is the 'paleomammalian brain', responsible for emotions. It corresponds to that in mammals.

3. The 'newest' brain is the 'neomammalian brain', responsible for language and reasoning. It corresponds to that of primates (including humans). The highest level of the brain is the neocortex. It includes the frontal lobes and other structures controlling higher cognitive processes. Remove this part of the brain, and the HS is left with the 'animal brain'. It means that in each human there is an animal deep inside. Or as Temple Grandin says, 'The animal brain is the default position for people when their frontal lobes are down'.[20]

This theory claims that each of these brains has its own intelligence and functions according to its own 'laws'. And here we come to the second issue of our discussion: size.

Yes, size does matter. Researchers agree that there is a correlation between brain size in relation to body size and the complexity of cognitive abilities. For instance, social insects (like ants and bees) have excess brain power relative to body weight.[21] Or take 'birdbrains': if we compare brain size relative to body size, the largest bird brains are larger than the smallest mammal brains.[22] Isn't it time to redefine the concept of 'birdbrain'?

In mammals the size of the neocortex is important. It is said that the bigger the neocortex, the more intelligent the creature. (But sometimes bigger brains may bring 'bigger problems' as well.) As animals and humans have different brains, their experiences of the world are different. However, despite all the differences, animal and human brains have a lot in common.[20] The same goes for autistic and non-autistic brains. No one doubts that autistic brains differ from non-autistic ones. However, all attempts to find one specific brain region that indicates autism have failed.[23] The first researcher who has come close to finding the structural differences in the autistic brain is the one whose name I couldn't remember earlier (though the name *is* famous). Now I can tell you (I checked it on the Internet), it is Dr Manuel Casanova. (Of course, Manuel Casanova has nothing to do with his famous name-sake, but everything to do with his ability to approach the problem with open mind.) Dr Casanova has found a striking difference in the brains of autistic individuals which distinguishes them not only from non-autistics but also from humans with other developmental disorders. Dr Casanova's team has identified the smallest units in the brain capable of processing information, which they named 'minicolumns'. They find that the brains of autistic humans have more numerous minicolumns and they are smaller in size than those of non-autistic brains. This has a dramatic effect on the way different parts of the brain interact with each other.[24]

Temple Grandin hypothesises that autistic humans' frontal lobes work differently from the frontal lobes of non-autistics. Autistic HSs use their 'animal brains' more than non-autistic individuals, because they have to. 'Autistic people are closer to animals than [non-autistic] people are'.[20] And that is why autism can help shed some light on the fascinating world of nHSs and vice versa, i.e. animals can aid in understanding the fascinating world of autism. Shall we proceed?

CHAPTER 5

'Senseless' and 'Senseful' Ways of Being

Let us start with a very popular assumption – 'Autistic children live in their own world.' I'm not meowing that this assumption is wrong, but I'd add several other statements to it: 'Non-autistic humans live in their own world', 'Blind humans live in their own world', 'Deaf humans live in their own world', 'Wild animals live in their own world', 'Domesticated animals live in their own world', 'Farm animals live in their own world', 'Cats live in their own world', etc. The list is endless. The fact is that there is one physical world (we are aware of), and as many 'sensory perceptual worlds' as there are different species. How do we all know what is 'out there'? We know through our senses, of course. It is our senses that 'deliver the information' about our environment, and our 'inner feelings' to the brain, where this raw information is processed, and 'our own world' is created. We then act upon it. This process is very complicated and differs greatly from species to species. This is why:

- the real world and different species' mental images of the world differ

- the interpretation of the world is based on memory and experience

- different sensory experiences create different perceptual worlds.

The same senses work differently in humans and animals. For instance, cat and human eyes both have rods (receptors sensitive to low light and sudden movements) and cones (colour receptors). But we cats have more rods than cones compared with humans, so we can see in the dark much better than HSs. We do see some colours – purple, yellow, blue and green, for example – but not as well as humans. The advantage of a restricted range of colour perception is that we cats can differentiate up to 25 different shades of grey.[1] Not that humans can appreciate this superior ability! For HSs grey is grey is grey. Besides, some animal senses do not necessarily correspond to human ones. Animals have some sensory receptors that are alien to HSs. These receptors let them see, hear and smell things that human animals cannot. For example, elephants have special sensors in their trunks, and probably on their feet as well, to detect vibrations. However, humans also have sensory receptors some animals don't.[2]

Do the senses of different species work differently? Absolutely. This brings us to the concept of 'umwelt' introduced by the nineteenth-century physiologist, Jacob von Uexküll.

Umwelt: the specific world of any given animal (humans included).

Can we know for sure what the umwelt of different animals is? No, we cannot. I, for one, don't know the umwelt of my friend Polly who is a Dalmatian dog. Despite the similarities of our colours (Mother sometimes calls me a 'Dalmatian cat'), Polly's umwelt is different from mine. For example, dogs in general do not have very good vision. Polly, being a good representative of all the canines, relies mostly on smell, as opposed to vision; it means her 'sensory world' is smellier than mine. And it is a million times smellier than that of humans.

Polly, a Dalmatian dog

Dasha, a 'Dalmatian cat'

I agree with HSs who accept that it is impossible to answer the philosopher Thomas Nagel's question 'What is it like to be a bat?'[3] But I would urge all the species to try to *imagine* the bat's (and any other species') umwelt and work from there. So far, the pessimistic conclusion ('we will never know what it is like to be a…') brings false assumptions about animals and humans and narrows the possibilities to understand each other better. I have developed several rules that have helped me to research this subject:

1. Don't think that the way you perceive the world is the only possible way to perceive it.

2. Learn how senses of different individuals (both human and non-human) work and use your imagination unrestricted with your own sensory faculties to reconstruct their umwelt.

3. Try to look at the world through their eyes, listen (in your imagination) to their auditory umwelt, experience their tactile sensations in your mind, etc. in order to reconstruct the umwelt of the person in question (either a HS or a nHS).

For example, what is the most important sense for bats? From the research we know it is their hearing. They hear ultrasound. Bats emit ultrasound waves from their mouths. Donald Griffin called the process by which bats navigate 'echolocation'.[4] It's difficult (impossible?) for HSs to comprehend because humans cannot hear what bats hear. But it is not impossible to study the bat (not in the laboratory but in its natural habitat), thus getting one step closer to understanding these particular creatures.

Speaking about senses, each species has developed the sensory systems they need to live in their natural environment. Evolution takes care of this. Many birds have remarkable eyesight, many predators possess extraordinary sense of smell, and so on. The importance of a given sense to an animal is reflected in the size of the neocortical area of the brain devoted to that sense. For example, cats have significant areas of the neocortex that are devoted to vision, hearing, touch and movement.[5] I don't have to be an ethologist (though I am!) to figure out that human brains are 'preoccupied' with other things, and their sense areas are smaller. In comparison to animals, human senses are poorly developed, so they miss a lot of information.

> *Ethologist:* a scientist who studies animal behaviour. The word ethology originated from Greek *ethos* (nature, disposition) and is not restricted to non-human animals, but includes *all* species (humans included). In this sense the best human ethologists are cats, who detect the patterns of each character very easily and use this knowledge to manipulate their humans.

Cats (and many other nHSs) perceive things humans can't perceive. From a felinological point of view, human senses are 'senseless'. Ninety-nine per cent of HSs seem to be nearly deaf! They hear just a few (loud) sounds in their environment and miss a lot of 'auditory information'. For example, they do not hear the clock ticking, the bicycle turning the corner, or the dog barking two blocks away. I don't know how they manage to survive relying just on a few sounds that must be quite loud to be heard by them. Concerning vision, HSs (even with 20/20 vision) are blind to 90–95 per cent of what is out there to see. I still cannot comprehend how they function without smelling their furniture and friends and recognise their surroundings by just a few visual cues. Their brains seem to ignore a lot of information available, and they do not notice such huge changes in their bedroom, for example, as a five-pence coin under the wardrobe or a piece of fluff on the carpet under the dressing-table. Sometimes I wonder – how can they find their way in their environment when it changes every day? They seem to *know* what is there, and never bother actually to look and to check. Compared to me, they miss a lot of information.

Cats' senses are *very* keen. Some HSs compare them to hypersensitivity in autism. However, for animals, this 'hyper-sensitivity' is normal. Strictly meowing, it is not 'hyper' at all.

The original error many HSs made was to concentrate all their efforts on treating hypersensitivities in autism as if they were the main problem. Very few human researchers could see that hypersensitivities of 'autistic senses' are consequences of other sensory perceptual differences in autism. Actually, sensory differences may be among the first signs of autism in young children and can be detected much earlier than social and communication impairments.[6]

I want to emphasise that not all the differences in perception are dysfunctional, and sensory differences are not necessarily problems or difficulties. Some may be interpreted as strengths or even superabilities that can become 'dysfunctional' if not recognised and accommodated by the outside world. It all depends on whether they are useful in particular environments. Sadly, non-autistic HSs cannot appreciate them because they don't know these abilities exist. Some difficulties may be caused by environmental factors. For example, if a person is hypersensitive to fluorescent lights, his or her 'dysfunction' will be noticeable only in rooms with fluorescent lighting. If this hypersensitivity is accommodated (replacing fluorescent tubes with low wattage light bulbs, for example), this particular 'dysfunction' will disappear.

There is an assumption that information acquisition is intact in autism and that the problems start at higher-level processing. Yes and No. Yes, they are not blind or deaf, but No, because their senses function differently. I'd like to introduce my first hypothesis: babies who would be diagnosed autistic have differences in their sensory functions. Their senses may be either 'too open', or 'not open enough'. (Don't take it literally. This is the best way I can express what I mean in humanese.) The 'openness' may bring both superabilities and deficits. It may lead to what Olga Bogdashina calls Gestalt perception – perception of the whole scene as a single entity with all the sensory details perceived (but not processed) simultaneously. (The only objection I have is the term 'Gestalt' to explain it. She writes in English, why use a German word? By the way, I have nothing against the German language, but it proves that she doesn't know English well enough to stick to one language at a time.) Another definition of Gestalt perception is 'the inability to distinguish between foreground and background sensory information; inability to filter it'. Autistic children seem to perceive everything without filtration or selection. This results in a paradoxical phenomenon: sensory information is received in tiny detail and holistically at the same time.[7]

For autistic children, each and every situation is unique. They can learn what to do in one situation but be lost if the slightest detail is different. Any tiny difference changes the whole situation. For example, our Alex corrects all the 'wrongs' the minute he enters the living room in the morning: he might pick up a piece of fluff from under the table, move the chair a few inches to the 'right position,' take Mother's mug to the kitchen, etc. For him, to function successfully everything should be 'right', i.e. the way it was yesterday, the day before yesterday, a week ago.

The good news is that Alex is becoming more flexible. A couple of years ago he would throw a tantrum if anything were out of order – for example, the picture was not straight on the wall, or his toy was on the chair instead of being on the window sill. As he didn't communicate what was wrong, how could his family see the trigger? Now Alex is quite happy to correct all the 'wrongs' himself.

The boy still has some difficulties, though. It is impossible to return from a walk with him without following exactly the same route and stopping at the same places the family has done before. It's OK if they walk to the shop – the whole family is well trained to cover the same ground to avoid any major accident. The problems start when they go shopping by a car. I don't know about other countries (I haven't travelled abroad yet), but in the UK road works seem to be a British institution – wherever and whenever they drive there are diverting arrows because road-workers are digging the holes one day and filling them up the next. For poor Alex and others like him it's very confusing if their car has to turn right, for example, when they are supposed to go straight ahead. Any unexpected turn becomes a threat; it brings anxiety – Are we going where they've said we're going? Those who live with autistic children learn very quickly to avoid too many changes or, if it's impossible, at least warn the child about what is going to change and why. Alex trained his family when he was still very young and non-verbal. One day his Dad took him to the shop and naively believed that as Alex knew this particular shop there wouldn't be any surprises. Wrong! They went in a car, and half way to the shop Dad remembered that he needed petrol to continue the journey, so he turned from the main road to the petrol station without telling Alex what he was going to do. Alex (naturally) panicked: he thought they were going shopping but his Dad was taking him somewhere else. (Wouldn't you panic if you didn't know what was going on around you and where you were being taken?) You don't want to know what happened next, but they never got to the shop. After this lesson, Alex is always provided with all the necessary information *before* the family goes out.

Our Alex has not only visual but also auditory Gestalt perception. He finds it extremely difficult to screen out irrelevant sounds. He cannot even decide which sounds are irrelevant to each given situation. All auditory information comes in as a package. When someone talks to him, Alex hears not only the voice of this person but also the movement of water in the pipes in the bathroom, the microwave working in the kitchen, the neighbour opening the gate, cars passing, me eating my tuna... The poor boy is very easily frustrated when he has to do something in a noisy, crowded place.

To feel safe, Alex creates 'Gestalt behaviours' – rituals and routines. These behaviours bring reassurance and order in his daily life which is otherwise unpredictable and threatening. These rituals may seem long and complicated to outsiders. However, for Alex, it is one act of meaningful experience, and if any part of it is missing (for example, he is prevented from completing a seemingly meaningless ritual), the whole experience becomes incomplete, unfamiliar and frightening. Our Alex has several rituals that are very important for him to function in a threatening (and disorganised) world of non-autistics. Before going to bed he has to touch all the doors and then straighten the pillows and blanket. It doesn't matter that when he actually gets into the bed the blanket loses the smoothness he has just created; he wouldn't get under the blanket if it were not 'right'. There is also a ritual of getting up in the morning. It's quite complicated, with certain movements and verbal exchanges with his mother. The 'script' of the morning ritual is played out every morning in exactly the same manner – up to the last word and movement. Fortunately, all the members of my family are 'autism professionals' by now. We all learned long ago – if we are in a hurry, never ever rush things with Alex or you'll have to wait for him for hours! If the boy was prevented from completing his highly elaborate ritual, for example, if Mum tried to skip several lines from her part of the 'morning scenario', Alex would get into bed again and start again from the very beginning.

Paradoxically, autistic HSs cope with big changes much better than with tiny ones. For example, when the family (minus me) go abroad on holidays (with me going to the kennel – the world is unfair!) Alex can cope in unfamiliar hotels. But if someone changes anything in his bedroom, Bastet and Sekhmet help us! The explanation lies in Gestalt perception. Alex's encounter with new information is a new Gestalt, which will be stored in his memory, while any changes in the familiar environment bring confusion: on the one paw, it becomes a completely 'new picture'; on the other paw, in the familiar situation he is confronted with an unfamiliar environment. I've noticed that structure and routine help Alex to understand what is going to happen, and when and why, and eventually he learns to accept little changes, especially when he is actively involved in changing the environment – tidying up his room, redecorating the house and so on.

Another strategy Alex's parents use to help him cope is giving him 'safety objects' in difficult situations or after a stressful event. Many autistic children are strongly attached to certain things: a piece of string, a twig, a wrapper, a spoon, a towel, a toy… The list is endless. For our Alex, it's a cuddly toy. For many years – actually since I came to live with this family – it was a toy reindeer, officially known as Rudolf, but called by Alex 'Gnome'. Gnome was not a mere toy – it was our saviour. Alex needed it when he went to bed, or in unfamiliar places, or after 'difficult times' in crowded situations. He did not play with his Gnome, he just held it in his hand or sometimes under his chin and…felt safe! Some (not very sapient) humans tell Mother that Gnome (or any other toy, for that matter) is not age-appropriate. Alex is a teenager now. But Mother knows better – she doesn't care about the politically correct age-appropriateness. (Oh, I love this woman!) She is absolutely right. Alex doesn't play with his cuddly toy in public, so it's not embarrassing and other humans do not stare. But he needs it when he needs it, especially when the family goes on holiday. They can sleep at night in any hotel as long as Alex has his 'safety object' with him. Sadly, after hundreds of times of going through a washing machine and a few dozens of patches, Gnome retired last year. It is in a very honourable place in Alex's bedroom but can't travel with him any more in case it falls apart. Now Alex's favourite is a toy elephant. It has passed the test – the elephant travelled to Greece last summer and the holiday was a success.

Being verbal thinkers, HSs never pay much attention to their sensory environment. They don't notice simple things, like shadows or colours, shapes or reflections, because they conceptualise and categorise everything or, as Temple Grandin says, non-autistic humans 'are abstractified in their sensory perception as well as their thoughts'. That is a big difference between animals and humans, and also between autistic and non-autistic humans.[8]

We cats memorise our environment and regularly inspect it to be sure that everything is in order. With these messy creatures around it's a hard job to adjust to all the changes they introduce the minute they enter the house. We cats trust nothing until we have checked on everything (using all the senses). For example, when I enter the room for the first time, I immediately switch on my 'primary devices' – hearing and smell – to assess the situation, with additional confirmation from my vision, touch and body-sense, and only then am I able to settle down in the hundredth version of the living room these 'senseless' HSs have created. I am very lucky to have a partner (Alex) who helps me to keep the house safe, and patiently (most of the time) corrects all the 'wrongs' imposed by the adults in our household.

Gestalt perception leads to 'literal' perception. 'Animals and autistic humans don't see their ideas of things; they see the actual things themselves.'[8] With age, non-autistic HSs' perception becomes even less accurate. Every time they look at something they just pick up a few features and recognise the whole picture from their past experiences and memories. For example, when Mother enters our living room she doesn't examine every object there to recognise it. She just knows what and where everything is located. A quick glance is enough. Unlike autistic individuals, non-autistics see more from the 'inside', from what is in their heads, than what is actually there outside of their mental world. Look, for example, at the picture. Can you see my friend Polly, a Dalmatian dog, in this picture?

If the answer is 'yes', then you have to check your vision! There is NO dog on the picture, nor any other animal, for that matter. This is a picture of black spots on the white background. Many humans impose meaning from their own memories to everything they look at, making their perception inaccurate. On the other paw, many autistics' perceptions are much more accurate, and in the non-autistic environment…dysfunctional. In the modern human world it's not good enough to see what is actually there. Instead, one should be able to impose an invented world on the physical reality.

Temple Grandin states that autistic people see the details that make up the world, while non-autistic individuals blur all the details together into their general concept of the world. Being the most famous visual thinker in the world, she explains that visual thinkers of any species, both animal and human, are detail-oriented, meaning that they see everything and react to everything. Tiny changes in their environment

Can you see a Dalmatian dog?

that 'senseless' HSs do not notice will jump out at visual creatures, and it is very disturbing for them.[8] I cannot agree more.
However, I'd add that this can be true not only about vision,
but about any sense, depending on which sense is dominant
or most reliable for each particular creature. For example,
Polly would react to any 'unsmellable' odour; it jumps at her.
But she wouldn't notice a twig or a coin on the floor, a few
inches from where she is sitting. My point is that not all
animals are visual and not all autistics are visual thinkers.
Those species whose vision is unreliable in comparison to

other senses would use other sensory modalities to interpret their world and reconstruct their mental image of it.

There is an additional reason for autistic individuals to 'insist on sameness': sensation lasts too long! Non-autistics 'forget' the sensation very quickly. For example, when you get dressed in the morning you can feel your clothes on your skin, but soon the feeling fades. This fading sensation is called habituation. It is the same with smell and taste, or any other sense. If the senses are exposed to a continuing stimulus, habituation soon occurs. When the stimulus changes, the feeling returns. That is why you do not feel the clothes you are wearing and become aware of them only if you change or adjust them.[7] For many autistic humans, however, the habituation process does not work properly and the sensation lasts too long. For some, it takes a few days to stop feeling their clothes on the body. And unfortunately, when this comfortable feeling (or 'no-feeling') has been achieved it is time to wear clean ones, so the process of getting used to the sensation starts again. The most difficult times are when they have to change from winter clothes to summer ones and the other way round. It takes weeks to get used to wearing shorts and short-sleeved tops. But by the time they feel comfortable enough to expose the skin, it's autumn and time to start wearing trousers and long-sleeved jumpers again.

Another (quite common) problem caused by their difficulty to stop feeling sensation is when their nails are being cut. Alex, for example, hates it as the process of 'cutting' doesn't stop when his mother finishes clipping his nails and puts the scissors away. It's not that the feeling of nails being cut remains, but rather that the surface of the cut nail is broader and makes it feel like the air is 'pressing on' the nails. The boy keeps feeling the sensation for at least three to four days. He tries to describe how it feels, but because of his differences in using the language, the best he comes up with is,

'My nails are sticky.' He feels better on the fifth or sixth day after the 'traumatic event', but the comfortable existence lasts only two more days when it's time to have his nails clipped again. I've found a very interesting and convincing explanation of this phenomenon in the research of Dr Casanova. His comparative studies of minicolumns in the brains of non-autistic and autistic individuals reveal that in non-autistic brains information is transmitted through the core of the minicolumn and is prevented from activating neighbouring units by surrounding inhibitory fibres. In autism, because minicolumns are so small and their number is so big, stimuli are no longer contained within them but rather overflow to adjacent units thus creating an amplifier effect. Inhibitory fibres just do not cope with this flow.[9] To illustrate this phenomenon, Dr Casanova compares inhibitory fibres with a shower curtain. When working properly and fully covering the bathtub, the shower curtain prevents water from spilling to the floor. In autism, 'water is all over the floor'.[10]

Gestalt perception and inability to stop experiencing sensations make autistic individuals vulnerable to sensory overload. I saw some carers making demands far exceeding their children's abilities to cope, just because they assume all babies can do this. Left to their own devices, autistic children develop their own adaptations and compensations very early in life. For example, to protect themselves from painful and confusing experiences, they may shut down their sensory systems, creating self-imposed sensory deprivation. (This strategy brings a relief but unfortunately the side effects can be unfavourable.[11]) When he was a toddler, Alex was suspected of being deaf because sometimes he didn't react to any (even very loud) sounds. His hearing, however, turned out to be very acute; he just learned to 'switch it off' when he couldn't cope with his 'sound environment'. Mother used to stand behind Alex and shout his name to attract his attention, with not even a blink from her offspring. But as soon as she started unwrapping a box of biscuits in the kitchen, Alex was by her side in no time at all. To shut down the painful channel(s), the boy might engage in stereotypic behaviours, or deliberately distract himself through other channels, for instance, touching objects to 'switch off' his vision or hearing, or withdraw altogether.

No one (even I) can guess that Alex's eyes, for example, pick up different signals from light, colour and movement. No one (but very few HSs and I, of course) can, however, imagine how each particular individual experiences the world through his or her senses. The trick is to be prepared to consider the possibility that what is 'normal' is different for different human and non-human animals.

When too much information needs to be processed simultaneously, very often humans with autism process only those bits which happen to get their attention. It seems as though they react to parts of objects as being whole things. As fragmented perception can affect all the senses, these 'bits and pieces' may be visual, auditory, olfactory, etc.[12] Alex (whose visual processing is fragmented) has great difficulty in dealing with people as not only do they seem to consist of many unconnected pieces but also the movements of these 'bits of people' are unpredictable. He hates it when someone points at something in front of him, because in this case 'a hand' (not 'his mother's or his teacher's hand') suddenly appears in front of his nose. What reaction would you expect from him with an unidentified object flying in the air? Of course, he wouldn't say 'Oh, hello, how are you?' (Would you, in a similar situation?) The best outcome is when he just shouts, 'Don't point!'; the worst... After one of these unfortunate accidents, Alex drew a picture of the person he had tried to hit in the shop.

Hands, hands, hands – everywhere

As Alex perceives his surroundings and humans he encounters in 'bits and pieces', he interprets and stores in his memory
his very individual (and idiosyncratic – from the non-autistic
point of view) impressions of his experiences. The boy recognises things and other humans by the 'sensory pieces' he has
stored as their definitions. For example, when he was a baby,
Alex recognised his mother by the red colour of her dress (at
the time she had a few gowns of her favourite red colour). Her
decision to change into a blue one led to her first encounter
with the police! Alex didn't recognise his mother and
screamed as if it were a matter of life and death. The frightened neighbours called the police. Later, they apologised for
letting their imagination paint a picture of murder – Alex's
screams suggested he might have been being tortured. This
incident is part of the family history which will be passed
from generation to generation.

Because of fragmented perception, HSs with autism seem to live in a different time zone because they may experience *delayed processing*.[13] For example, Alex may be able to repeat what has been said without comprehension; that will come later when he will make an announcement irrelevant to the situation. For outsiders it looks weird. We – those who live with him – however, can actually connect the 'announcement' with the question one of the humans asked last month, a week, or a couple of hours ago. Alex may need some time to process the question and prepare his response. Before a proper response Alex may go through a number of separate stages, and if he is interrupted by somebody who (on the surface) tries to help him by repeating the question (but actually distracts him), the poor boy must start all over again because the same question seems a new one for Alex.

Hypersensitivities to sensory stimuli are very common in autism. The senses of autistic humans may be too acute, and they may be disturbed by something that does not bother non-autistic humans. For instance, certain things they touch may hurt their hands. Certain noises may hurt their ears. This is true not only of loud sounds; sometimes the most disturbing sounds for an autistic individual are those that cannot be heard by non-autistic humans.[14]

As I've already mentioned, autistic hypersensitivities are sometimes compared to animals' senses. This comparison is both right and wrong. Right – because some individuals, like some animals, can see, hear, smell, feel stimuli that other humans wouldn't notice. Wrong – because for animals it is their normal perception, but for autistic individuals this hypersensitivity may be disturbing and even painful. Animals' senses are designed to function in their environment, while for autistic individuals their senses may be too sharp for the environment in which they live. The acuteness of 'autistic senses' becomes a problem because other HSs do not experience it and the environment is not designed to accommodate the hypersensitivity – non-autistic HSs are not bothered by the stimuli that are painful for some autistic humans. But even if all non-autistic HSs decided to take into account autistic hypersensitivities, it wouldn't solve the problem: autistic humans are very different and their sensitivities are unique. What is painful and disturbing for some may be pleasurable for others.

Autistic senses may be *hyposensitive* too. Sometimes not enough stimulation comes in, and they are deprived of sights, sounds, smells, etc. They cannot clearly see or hear the world around them, or even feel their own body. Some with *hypoproprioception* may have no concept of their bodies because they have never experienced it. For Alex's friend, David, his body is... a reflection in the mirror! Dave has never felt pain or temperature. To stimulate his senses and get at least some meaning out of what is going on, David waves his hands around, or rocks, or jumps up and down.[15]

It would be too easy to identify which senses are hyper and which ones are hypo and think you could solve the problem, but (repeat after me) whatever autism is, it's never boring! One and the same individual may experience both hyper- and hyposensitivity of the same sensory modality at different times. Fluctuation of the 'volume' of their perception is quite common in autism. The inconsistency of receiving information, when the sensations are changing day to day, hour to hour, and even minute to minute doesn't help the learning of social and emotional cues from other humans.[16]

Both autistic and non-autistic HSs have the same seven senses, but the way they use them is very different. Non-autistic HSs use all their senses simultaneously. For instance, they can see what is in front of them, listen to the radio and move to the music, all at the same time. For many autistic HSs it's too much. To limit the amount of information and avoid overload and fragmentation, they may use one sensory channel at a time, while the rest of the senses are on hold. This brings certain restrictions in their perception but helps to make sense of what is going on, in at least one sensory modality. For example, Alex's preferred channel is hearing. It is through sounds that he understands what is happening around him. He hears every noise in his environment, but he loses track of his other senses, so he doesn't make much sense of the sights around him, and loses the feel of touch or body awareness. Sometimes he is unable to process information produced from the outside and the inside at the same time. How do I know? I conducted a well-planned experiment. Last Monday, Alex was sitting in the living room, deep in his 'sound world' – he was listening to what was going on in the kitchen. Mother was laying the table – oops – she dropped a fork, picked it up and threw it into the washbasin, took another one from the drawer… That's when I jumped on his knee. Not a blink, Alex was too involved in his 'auditory world' to notice my presence – his tactile system and vision were off. Two minutes passed and – 'Aaaahhh! Dasha is on my knee!' He was so startled, as if I had materialised out of thin air. I don't like screaming, but if you are a scientist sometimes you have to be prepared to sacrifice yourself!

His friend Mike's main channel is touch. The boy can do wonders with his hands. His mother has taught him to read giving him plastic letters to feel. The progress was so good that Michael was accepted into a mainstream school. That's where the disaster struck. Whenever Mike was absorbed in his tactile world, doing all the activities through touch, his teacher (with the best intentions!) would say, 'Look at what you are doing!' After each (unhelpful) reminder to switch on his vision, Mike reacted with aggression, and his grades went downhill. In a few months Mike was expelled from his school and since then he has been educated at home.

Another strategy Alex uses to avoid overload and get meaning from the outside world is *peripheral perception*. He hates eye contact – it hurts![17] I've noticed that Alex actually hears his parents better if he is not looking at them. When he is in his bedroom upstairs and his parents are discussing something downstairs, the boy absorbs this information with precision and understanding. His mother knows his strategy, and uses it to talk to her son. For example, when they are in the same room and she wants to tell him something, she talks to... the wall. It's amazing how fruitful and interactive their conversation becomes. Lisa talks to her brother via his toy elephant. The results are great, as well. This is what Donna Williams calls the indirectly confrontational approach in contrast to a 'normal' directly confrontational one.[18] It's a pity that some professionals do not see it this way and start any interaction with an autistic child with 'Look at me!' Illogical, isn't it? First they make the child shut down and then attempt to teach him. Why eye contact is more important than meaningful conversation is beyond me.

Some autistic HSs seem to be hypersensitive when they are approached directly by other humans or animals. For some, if they are looked at directly, they may feel it as 'a touch' – sort of 'distance touching' with actual tactile experience. When I'm bored I play my favourite game with Alex (which is also useful for my research): I sit in front of Alex and look at him directly. It's so exciting to listen to his 'Dasha is looking at me! Tell her turn away! Tell her turn away!' The second stage of this game is even more fun – Mother's attempts to negotiate with me.

Autistic humans with peripheral perception often seem to look past things and appear to be completely 'absent' from the scene. However, it could be their attempt to avoid experiencing visual or auditory stimuli directly. This strategy gives them the ability to take in sensory information with meaning.

Some HSs are unaware of this clever adaptation. They feel free to discuss their personal affairs in the presence of autistic children who *seem* to be in their own world, for example, sitting in the corner, rocking and flapping their hands in front of their eyes. There have been so many entertaining moments, when our Alex came home from school, repeating whole conversations verbatim. He might not understand the whole conversation but he was able to repeat it at ease. (Of course, I'm not disclosing his support staff's secrets – I'm a professional researcher and, though tempting, I try not to be interested in who, when, what, with whom.)

During my recent catnap, when I was conducting my passive research, I realised why one sense is never enough for some autistic HSs to make sense of their environment. For instance, if their vision is unreliable, they might use their ears, nose, tongue or hand to 'see'. A person may tap objects to hear the sound it produces and recognise what it is. For many autistic children the senses of touch and smell are most reliable. Some children may smell humans and objects to identify them. Of course, these behaviours do not look normal to non-autistics, and they do their best to eradicate them – 'Stop smelling people. It is not nice!' But if smell is the only reliable sense for the child, isn't it more productive to address the problems of 'unreliable senses' (for example, providing tinted glasses to help eliminate visual fragmentation and hypersensitivity)? This will make 'inappropriate' strategies (like smelling) redundant. Alex used to smell his food before he was confident that it was something he liked. When his visual problems were addressed (he's been wearing his tinted glassed since he was eight), he stopped smelling things.

I have to mention another condition that is not specific to autism but seems to be quite common in ASDs. It is face-blindness, or prosopagnosia. (It took me a couple of days to remember this word. I could have just said 'face-blindness', but if I want to be a researcher I'd better learn to use difficult words as well.) Face-blindness makes people 'blind' to all but the most familiar faces. They do *see* faces, but fail to recognise them; all faces are just faces, not Mr X's face and Mrs Y's face. Some face-blind humans find themselves in very embarrassing situations when they do not react to their friends passing them on the street because they don't recognise them. Quite a few autistic humans have this condition as well. Some researchers suggest that prosopagnosia may be an essential symptom in ASDs, perhaps a specific group of Asperger syndrome.[19] I'm so interested in this new to me condition, because three members of my adopted family are prosopagnostic: Mother, Alex and Lisa. While Mother and Lisa try to hide it from their friends (what can I say about female humans' logic?), Alex has a more straightforward and practical approach: the first question he asks whoever he meets is 'What is your name?' A very good strategy. The answer he gets tells him whether he knows this person or it's somebody he has never met before.

The problem for many autistic HSs is that they don't realise that they perceive the world differently from the other 99 per cent of HSs, because they have nothing to compare their perception with. They may think that other HSs are better and stronger than they are when they cannot tolerate scratchy clothes or loud noises, for example. Or they may sometimes think that other humans are shallow and non-appreciative of the beauty of colours, sounds and textures. However, a bigger problem is that HSs around them are unaware of their different perception and do not make any effort to understand and accommodate these differences. Non-autistic humans seem to think their perception is a perfect one and everybody has the same experiences. If somebody behaves differently from the 'norm' they are quick to doubt the person's intelligence. The ignorance of some not very sapient HSs doesn't know any boundaries. It's difficult to believe, but some humans don't know that they don't know!

When I want to understand my humans, I try to imagine how the world looks through their eyes, sounds through their ears, feels through their skin and body, smells through their nose, tastes through their tongue. In short, I try to understand how they *experience* the world through their senses. When I started my research, I asked myself a question: What is it like to be Alex? Though it is impossible to get the exact answer to this question, it is possible to imagine what Alex may be seeing/hearing/feeling. Alex's mother has learned a lot from me. (I have taught her to make the home Dasha-friendly.) Through her experience with meeting my needs, she has learned how to identify Alex's umwelt and now knows what things are scary for Alex, what things and activities he loves doing, and the concerns he has. The family has adjusted the environment at home to make him feel safe and started the programme to desensitise Alex to his sensitivities. It's a very wise decision because they won't be able to change the outside world to meet his needs. As best as I can, I urge them not to stop here. They have to understand not only the way Alex perceives the world around him but also how he interprets it and how he communicates, because differences in perception lead to development of different abilities, thinking styles, manifestation of emotions, language and communication.

CHAPTER 6

Thinking
about Thinking

Since I started my research I've been thinking about… thinking. As I prefer to base all my studies on a sound philosophical ground, I start with René Descartes' principle establishing the existence of a being from the fact of its thinking or awareness – 'Cogito ergo sum' or 'I think, therefore I am.' I know that 'I am' – I'm alive, aren't I? I know that I think, but when Polly asked me what thinking meant I had to think before I could answer my friend's question. The fact is that humans often use several words to describe one and the same notion. They call them synonyms.

> *Synonyms*: two or more (very different) words with the same meaning, e.g., 'cat', 'puss' and 'feline' mean 'Dasha' (i.e. me). The meaning is the same but sometimes synonyms may differ in neutrality/formality and emotional colouring. For instance, when you approach me as a researcher it's better to call me 'feline'; if you don't want to be too formal, you may call me a 'cat'. My family and my friends may call me Dasha. (Don't call me 'puss' – I don't like it!)

The other word for thinking in human vocabulary is cognition. Eventually, I came up with these definitions:

Thinking: using thoughts.

Cognition: a general term for mental processes by which sensory information is interpreted, stored and used.

Theoretically, these two words are interchangeable and mean the same, but, illogically, some HSs insist that, while discussing animals, it is useful to distinguish between 'thinking' and 'cognition'. They define *cognition* as processes by which sensory input is transformed, reduced and elaborated, and *thinking* as attending to the animal's internal mental images or representations. They say that many animals can cognate (i.e. get sensory information and store it in their memory) but are unable to *think* because they have only a very simple level of consciousness.[1] In other words, non-human animals do think but they don't know that they think! Who is doing the thinking then?

The main argument some HSs use to deny us ability to think is that, if animals have no verbal language, they cannot think. This is one of the most ridiculous ideas I've come across. Fortunately some scientists are clever enough to see the absurdity of this assumption. The German ethologist Otto Koehler has demonstrated that animals display 'wordless thinking' with regard to quantity. (At least it's a start. Soon, I hope, more humans will get used to the idea that 'wordless thinking' may be about quality as well.) Koehler found that some animals can 'see numbers': they choose the object with a certain number of points on it from among a group of objects with points differing in number, size, colour and arrangement and 'act upon a number' (by repeating an act a certain number of times). Koehler's research has established that the upper limit of both 'seeing numbers' and 'acting' on them for pigeons was five points, for parakeets and jackdaws six, for ravens, Amazons, grey parrots, magpies and squirrels, seven. The animals were able to translate a heard number into a seen one: to select a seven-dotted dish from others on hearing seven whistles, drum beats, or flashes of light.[2]

I'm not suggesting that humans will ever understand animal thoughts in their entirety – it's just impossible – but do humans understand their own thinking? How can any human understand the thinking processes in their entirety while being not only the object of the process but also the subject of it? Does that make sense? Sometimes I can't express what I want to meow; the humanese doesn't contain the words to describe some of my feline experiences. Why can't HSs just admit that nHSs possess some type of self-consciousness, the nature of which cannot be described in full detail?

The best evidence of conscious thinking and feeling in animals is their actions. Donald Griffin believes that conscious thought is the most economical explanation of animal behaviour. Animals have to adapt constantly to a changing environment. They are not passive objects; their thinking is rational and conscious.[3] Simple perceptual and rational conscious thinking is as important for small animals (myself included) as for those with large brains.[4] The difference seems to lie in the level of consciousness. There are several suggestions as to how to classify consciousness from simple to complex level depending on the complexity of the brain. For my analysis I've opted to distinguish several types of consciousness:

- Simple consciousness: common in insects.

- Higher consciousness, that in turn may be subdivided into several levels of consciousness. Humans, with the most complex brains, have a higher level of consciousness than, for example, dogs, which have smaller, less complex brains but have consciousness nevertheless.[5] Ethologists and cognitive psychologists (some very reluctantly) agree that animals have some consciousness (primary consciousness) because animals do get sensory information and act on it, but unlike humans, they are not self-aware.

- Self-consciousness or self-awareness: HSs are said to have this level of consciousness. They experience some entity – 'I' – that thinks about its own thinking. I'd call it the feeling of 'I-ness'.

I-ness (Synonyms: self-consciousness, self-awareness): awareness of being 'I' and experiencing of being alive, doing things and perceiving what is happening to 'I'.

The question is, do nHSs have such self-consciousness? I-ness may have several forms. The simplest is experiencing what one is doing. When, for example, I see a mouse, I know how to perform my hunting technique: first I scan the environment for any cover (the later the mouse sees me the better), and then, with my body very low, I run forwards, stop to prepare for the attack, with my body still very close to the ground; my hind paws move on the spot, my tail's tip twitching. My eyes are on the target all the time. When the moment is right, I launch my attack. Soon my (ungrateful) pets are presented with my contribution to the meal. They don't really appreciate it, especially Mother. Instead of praising my accomplishment, she jumps on whatever piece of furniture is the nearest to her and screams at the top of her voice: 'Anyone, please remove the body!' What can I say? Women.

Donald Griffin supports my views (even without knowing about my existence!). He states that it is reasonable to attribute this type of consciousness to mammals and birds, on the same basis as it is attributed to young pre-linguistic children.[3] Animals' nervous systems may be simple, but conscious and rational; nHSs are able to think about alternative actions and choose those the animals believe will get what they want, or avoid what they dislike or fear.

Another type of consciousness is what Professor Susan Armstrong-Buck calls 'public self-consciousness'.[6] This is the awareness the person experiences as he or she is seen (and judged) by the public. I'm not very experienced in this. I do feel when others (either HSs or nHSs) stare at me, but I don't like it. And I don't care what they think about me. Why should I?

The public self-consciousness is a social experience. For example, chimps reared in isolation seemed incapable of self-recognition in the mirror experiments,[7] while those who live with others easily learn to recognise themselves. Dr Patterson found lots of evidence for self-awareness in gorillas, including recognising themselves in a mirror, use of self-referential words, linguistic descriptions of feeling, and behaviour indicating embarrassment.[8]

I've learned about this type of self-consciousness from a friend of mine (and of the family), a lady with Asperger syndrome, also known as Miss Ponytail. After a couple of hours in public our friend is exhausted. She hates all the attention (real and imagined) and spends a few days in solitude 'to restore her sanity', she says. And it was believed that humans on the autism spectrum do not care how others react to them! It may be true for some humans with autism, but Miss Ponytail and some other HSs with ASDs are very well aware of public presence in their lives. Many a time this awareness brings a very uncomfortable feeling and physical exhaustion. It's from Miss Ponytail that I heard about yet another type of self-consciousness: 'pure self-consciousness'. Miss Ponytail described her earliest experiences of this (very difficult for me to comprehend) notion. I can't meow it better than she did, so I'll quote from memory: 'When I was very young (before age three, I'm sure, because I remember my bedroom very vividly, and my family moved houses when I was two years and a half) I used to lie in bed at night *feeling* me – not my physical body, but something that was *me*. Sometimes I was scared when the question emerged – "who am I?" I knew I could get the answer only if I followed this elusive "me" deeper inside, but I never finished this journey – I was too frightened, and always stopped in the middle to return back. These experiences were very scary but also fascinating at the same time. I never told my parents or anybody else till now. I think this is pure consciousness. Religious people would call it "soul".'

I'd like to mention another very interesting type of 'autistic consciousness'. Some autistic humans may have what Donna Williams calls fluctuation between 'all self–no other' and 'all other–no self'. In the state of 'all self–no other' the person knows what he or she feels, and wants to say or do, but is unable to get any meaning out of the environment – processing just sound or colour or movement; and in the state 'all other–no self' the individual is able to understand what is going on and what people are saying but can't reply because there is 'no self' – thoughts and feelings are unavailable at the moment.[9, 10]

Temple Grandin describes several levels of consciousness where different degrees of consciousness depend on the ability of different brain subsystems to integrate information and make associations.[5] Grandin's approach has a potential to account for many phenomena in self-awareness of both human and non-human animals:

- *Consciousness within one sense.* This type of consciousness explains why the 'mirror test' does not work with some animals. Those animals that do not recognise themselves in the mirror do not lack self-consciousness but rather may lack 'visual self-consciousness'. They are self-aware in other sensory modalities, for example, tactile-aware, or smell-aware. Some animals may be 'one-sense conscious'. Some autistic humans with severe sensory processing problems may experience difficulty in certain-sense self-consciousness but be aware in others. For instance, humans with proprioceptive problems may have a hard time to figure out their body boundary, especially when they experience sensory overload. They function much better in 'mono', where the most reliable sense brings meaning of what is going on around them. Some can switch channels and 'check' the information from different sensory modalities but have problems integrating stimuli from several senses simultaneously.

- *Consciousness where all sensory systems are integrated.* This type of consciousness is typical for many humans (both non-autistic and autistic ones) whose sensory systems are integrated. Temple Grandin places herself in this category because her thoughts are not connected with emotions.

- *Consciousness where all sensory systems are integrated with emotions.* Some humans with emotion recognition/expression problems may have difficulty with this level of consciousness.

- *Consciousness where sensory systems and emotions are integrated and thinking is verbal.* This type is very common in non-autistic HSs. However, lack of abstract language consciousness does not make it inferior to the 'highest consciousness' of humans with language thinking. 'Non-language thinkers' do have *mental language* that is qualitatively different from the conventional one.

Now, when I have found out who is doing the thinking, it's time to look at the thinking itself: development of mental languages, storing the information in the memory and manipulating mental images – thoughts.

When human babies are born they cannot talk. They do not come into this world greeting their mothers, midwives and other humans who are present at birth with cheerful 'Hello, everybody! How are you doing?' All their earliest experiences are sensory. With development and interaction with those around them, human babies develop their systems of interpretation of sensory input, wrapping sensory experiences up into verbal thoughts and learning to label them with words. Does this mean that before emergence of verbal thoughts babies do not think? Of course not. They do think. They have 'pre-verbal thoughts' that serve them well at that stage. These 'pre-verbal thoughts' (let's call them 'sensory percepts') do not disappear, and they are not replaced with verbal concepts.

> *Percept*: a mental image resulting from perceiving. For example, a visual image of me (visual percept), or the feeling of my fur on the hand (a tactile image), or the sound of my purring (auditory image) when the word 'cat' is heard.

> *Concept*: an abstract idea or mental image of a group or class of objects formed by combining their aspects. For example, cats of different colours, breeds, sizes (like Dasha, Sally, MtheD, etc.) all go under the same heading, 'a cat'.

Both sensory and verbal thoughts develop alongside each other as two interactive ways of knowing about the world. In human non-autistic development, verbal ways of knowing become dominant, and sensory percepts 'go underground' – they do not disappear completely and sometimes may be felt by some humans who describe these elusive feelings of knowing that something is wrong or right as 'gut feelings'. The majority of humans forget about their primary system of knowing by the time they develop verbal language, but many autistic HSs rely on this system much longer, sometimes well into their adulthood, or even all their lives. Those non-verbal autistics have a highly developed primary system of thinking that is invisible to others but could have been very efficient if their ways of knowing and functioning had been understood by other humans.

It is quite typical for HSs to label whatever they cannot understand as either 'primitive' or 'abnormal'. Is it a surprise then that anyone with different functioning is seen as inferior to 'normal' humans? Wouldn't it be better to learn from differences and enrich the lives of all the species with obtained knowledge and respect? Those without verbal language (here I mean non-human animals – what is the point of them having a verbal language, anyway?) are not primitive; they are very well equipped to live very productive lives in their own habitat. Their cognitive abilities are well developed, including sophisticated ways of thinking, using their 'mental words' with the ability to categorise their experiences. For example, Professor John Pearce devised tests to identify abilities to categorise in pigeons. The tests show that pigeons are capable of learning relatively abstract classificatory systems. The birds were able to select pictures with trees. They recognised not one particular tree, but a general concept of 'tree'. And it was not their excellent visual memory that let them complete the task. When they were presented with pictures they had never seen, the score of correct answers was much higher than chance: the pigeons demonstrated their ability to form concepts (the concrete concepts based on the images in their brains).[11] This shows that it is possible to develop concepts and thinking systems that are not dependent on verbal language.

Back to humans now. Non-autistic children learn to form categories and generalise. They unite things (not identical but serving the same function, for example) under the same label. They store concepts (not perceptual images and experiences). These concepts become filters through which all sensory experiences are filtered and organised into classes, groups and types. All sensory information seems to be forced to fit into the most likely interpretation based on their prior knowledge.[12] The outside world becomes conceptualised, represented and expressed in words that can be easily operated to create new ideas. Cognitive processes become more efficient and rapid because they allow humans to 'jump' from a very few perceptual details to conceptual conclusions. For example, many HSs will see the letter 'E' in a picture, though it is not there. This is the picture of lines. However, many HSs would 'jump' to the conclusion, because it easily fits into their concept of 'E'.

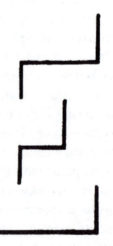

Letter 'E' or lines?

In contrast, many autistic humans perceive everything without filtration and selection and experience the difficulty of distinguishing between foreground and background sensory stimuli. That is why they often have difficulty moving from sensory patterns (literal interpretation) to understanding of functions and forming verbal concepts. For some, with severe sensory processing problems, verbal language may be merely noise that has nothing to do with either interaction or interpretation of the environment. Words do not mean anything; they are just sounds like the sound of running water, dogs barking, cars moving, etc. However, this does not mean that they remain stuck at the early stage of development (before acquiring verbal concepts). They do develop but 'via a different route'.[13] With the sensory-based system being dominant, the sensory impressions they store in their memory become templates for recognition and identification of things, people, events. The 'sensory concepts' are literal: everything is 'the' something. For example, if a child remembers a 'cat' as a small silver Persian with a white spot on its head, any other feline (even a Persian with a yellow spot) cannot be identified as a cat – it is so different! On the other paw, there are 'sensory synonyms': if different objects feel/smell, etc. the same they become identical 'words'.

Another example of difficulty to form verbal concepts in autism is described by Temple Grandin.[14] I have to write about it here to make it fair for my friend Polly. She is not very happy with me writing mostly about my kin; I don't want to lose my friend, so here it goes. Temple Grandin had problems trying to understand things like why a very small dog is not a cat, because all the dogs she knew (and stored in her memory) were big, so she distinguished between cats and dogs by size. (It would work for me and Polly: Polly is pretty big, and I am small in comparison.) But one day the neighbours bought a dachshund and Temple found it difficult to believe that it was a dog. It was too small for a dog. What was going on? She studied and studied that dachshund, trying to solve the puzzle. Finally – bingo! She realised that the dachshund had the same kind of nose as her golden retriever did. All dogs (both big and small) have dog noses.[14]

An interesting theoretical explanation of this phenomenon has been put forward by Professor Allan Snyder and colleagues: autism is the state of delayed acquisition of concepts.[15] The researchers argue that humans are not conscious of the details of percepts. Instead HSs often see what they expect to see or what is closer to their mental representations.[16] It is the object labels that are important, as they give them the idea of what is there without any need to be aware of all the details. On the other hand (I have to use this anthropomorphic expression because it's from the work by humans), certain individuals (for example, autistic savants) appear to have the opposite strategy. They have privileged access[17] to non-conscious information but are not concept-driven.[18]

While I'm at it, concepts can help to prevent sensory overload and decrease confusion. I've noticed that Mother's strategy to give labels in difficult situations helps Alex to 'fight his panic'. Providing a 'name' for the chaotic environment really explains a lot to the boy and is a good tool for him to figure out what is going on.

The differences in sensory perception of autistic HSs are reflected in peculiarities of their memory and thinking. Let's start with the ways they remember things. My conclusion is: the main characteristics of 'autistic memory' seem to be literalness (remembering things the way they are) and Gestalt where the 'items' (whole episodes of the situations) are not 'condensed', not filtered, not categorised, not summarised for a gist. Whereas conceptual memory typical for non-autistic humans is about remembering events and ignoring small irrelevant situations, Gestalt memory (in whichever modality

it works – visual, auditory, tactile, proprioceptive) is characterised by undistinguished equality of all the stimuli – the
large and small, the relevant and irrelevant all get the same
prominence.[13] The advantage of this is that the memory is
very (and I do mean *very*) good.

This morning I told Polly about my explorations of 'autistic memory', and Polly, being Polly, asked the question – the
answer to which is quite obvious if she knew the way autistic
HSs receive and process information – 'If their memory is
very good, why can't they answer the simplest question? For
example, when Mother asks Alex "What did you do at school
today?", the best she can get from him is either "I don't know"
or "I don't remember."'

The answer is Gestalt! If they remember whole situations
as single entities, to retrieve information to answer a question
they would have to 'play' the whole piece in their memory to
'find' the right 'word' (image, situation, etc.). Considering
their difficulties with verbal language it is no wonder they
find it hard to give the answer. However, if the 'interrogator'
provides them with the right trigger they may find the
relevant piece and may even be able to repeat whole conversations they have heard (even if they haven't processed them
yet). Mother learned her lesson long ago, and now before
asking Alex about his day she reads notes left by the teacher in
Alex's 'home-school book' and poses the right question, for
example, 'You went shopping with so-and-so in the morning.
What did you buy?' Alex recites his shopping list immediately
and adds other relevant information – 'Bubble bath costs
three pounds and ninety-nine pence!'

The same goes with thinking – in autism it is perceptual.
The most common type of perceptual thinking in autism is
visual. Visual thinkers actually *see* their thoughts. For them,
words are like a second language. In order to understand what
is being said to them or what they are reading they have to

translate it into images. It is visual thinking that helps Temple Grandin to understand animals' behaviour. She explains that animals are visual creatures, and they are controlled by what they see.[14] While I agree with this statement in principle, I'd add two points. First, not all animals are visual. What visual images go through the head of a bat, for example? Or, take Polly, a representative of canines; her world is constructed mostly of 'smell pictures', 'auditory images' and 'kinaesthetic ideas' with visual mode being a back up. Second, it's not enough to look in the same direction or from the same angle as visual animals do; it's also important to imagine what they *see* – animal and human visual systems work differently. Temple Grandin can do it because her perceptual processes differ from non-autistic abstract processing, but if, for example, Dad dropped on all fours to try to see our living room from my perspective, he would fail miserably. He would miss, for instance, the shadows on the carpet and a baby spider hiding behind the curtain.

Contrary to recent stereotype, not all autistic HSs think in pictures. In fact, those with severe visual perceptual problems have great difficulty in easily retrieving mental pictures in response to words.[19] Instead, they may use auditory, kinaesthetic or tactile images. Many may not actually be able to visualise and may be deprived of what could work for them, and their intelligence is then wrongly judged by their inability to link visual images with words.[20] That's exactly what happened to our Alex. He attends a school for children with autism. The school policy is to use pictures and symbols with their students irrespective of whether some students are unable to visualise. I always admire those autistic humans who learn to overcome not only the difficulties created by autism, but also human-made obstacles. Alex eventually learned to interpret the symbol of 'geometric shapes' as 'dinner'! Instead of using his 'tactile language' (for example, giving him a spoon five minutes before a meal), the boy was presented with a picture of a circle (allegedly known as a plate) and several sticks with different endings (supposedly representing a knife, a fork and a spoon). Wouldn't it be easier for everybody to choose the means to help autistic children interpret what is going on that match their internal language than using one system with all the children in the classroom? Alex's friend Michael is 'kinaesthetic' in his thinking. He is unable to interpret the spoken language without gestural signing. He uses his hands, feet and the whole body to understand and express himself.

I would have left it at that but Polly interferes yet again with her question: 'If Mike is a kinaesthetic thinker, why doesn't sign language work for him? His teachers have tried to introduce Makaton at school and this strategy failed miserably.' Sometimes I think that Polly is as blind to the obvious as most humans are. Makaton (or any other sign language) is based on verbal symbols that are too abstract for Mike and others like him. For example, how can he *feel* 'biscuit' when someone taps one's elbow? When Mike wants a biscuit he puts his hand to his mouth and makes a 'biting movement'. Polly wasn't satisfied with my explanation: 'But it can mean anything edible, not only a biscuit! How can humans know what Mike wants?'

'They can offer him a few choices – apples, biscuits, oranges and a sandwich, for example, and let him choose. Surely, miming is better than an abstract sign language not only for Michael but also for other humans who are not familiar with Makaton. Can you imagine the confusion of a shop assistant with Mike standing at the counter, tapping his elbow?'

Thanks to this internal (very real) language, autistic humans can experience thought as reality. It means that when they think about something, they relive it visually, auditorily and emotionally. O'Neill compares it with watching a movie: the pictures of thoughts in this mind movie create emotions as well while the scenes are playing.[21] Alex often giggles to himself. One of the reasons might be because he relives some funny moment, using recorded, stored sensory images. But sometimes Alex giggles when he is confused or scared by all the emotions around him. He used to giggle very loudly when his mother was upset and crying. The boy wasn't cruel (as some ill-informed humans suggested); he was frightened and very upset. At least his mother knows how to distinguish between (happy) giggling and (sad) giggling.

Autistic children are concrete thinkers. They have trouble with words that cannot be translated into mental images (whether visual, kinaesthetic, tactile, etc.) and often have problems learning abstract things that cannot be imagined via the perceptual mode. How can you see, or feel, or smell something like 'peace' or 'love' or 'of', for example? How can you translate 'social experiences' into the sensory mode? Instead of looking for answers and solutions, some non-autistic HSs prefer the label 'socially impaired'. It is easy, but is it fair?

Polly was very much involved in my research and asked the right questions when I was stuck. Together we've found out who is doing the thinking ('I') and what thoughts look like (verbal concepts in non-autistic humans and perceptual images in autistic HSs). The next step is to study how thoughts unfold, or how 'I' manipulates images/ideas while doing the thinking. And there is a need to understand linear, spatial and associative thinking patterns. Verbal thinking is linear: first I did this, then I went there, etc. Autistic thinking, in contrast, is spatial – when thoughts unfold in all directions simultaneously. This picture by an autistic boy is a very good illustration of visual spatial thinking.

Being a spatial thinker means that a person represents things in the mind with a multi-sensory, multi-dimensional

Spatial thinking

model. I'm a spatial thinker. That's why I find it very hard to express my thoughts in writing. I do my best to pull all my ideas into one line but they keep stretching in other directions. The only way to show my meaning is to use brackets, dashes and semicolons. If you want to have a go – try to describe what the spatial thinking picture above is all about.

Autistic thinking is also associative. One thought (or one 'image-word') leads to another that may be absolutely disconnected from the topic of conversation, but very logical in a different dimension. An illustration of associative thinking is a recent conversation the family had, when Lisa had another go at persuading her parents to enlarge our happy family with…a dog. The girl has been nurturing this idea for many months, and each time she tried new arguments to convince them. (I'm absolutely furious about her idea. I'm not against dogs in general, and Polly is my friend, but I don't want to share *my* territory and *my* humans even with her, to say nothing about other canines. This digression is not necessary for the discussion but I want my views known. It's a pity that my mates are unaware of them because we always have trilogues when they ignore my contributions to their conversations. Life is unfair.)

After a sleepover at her friend's, Lisa came home full of news. This is the transcript of the conversation illustrating associative thinking patterns, with my trilogical contributions and research notes.

Lisa: Kelly's parents have given her a Pekinese puppy as her birthday present. [Me: *Don't you start. Not again.*] It's the cutest –

Alex: (interrupting her) Umka jumped at Alex. I didn't want to break the teapot. It was an accident.

Lisa: (understanding her brother very well and knowing what he was talking about) It's the cutest puppy I've ever seen. And they have two cats, too!

Alex: Two plus two is four!

Lisa: Alex, don't interrupt.

Dad: Lisa, we've had this conversation before. You know the answer.

Lisa: Dasha needs some company. She is soooooo lonely. [Me: *I am not!*]

Lisa: She is friendly with Polly. It means –

Alex: Polly put the kettle on, Polly put the kettle on… I don't like tea. I like Coca-Cola!

Research notes: *Associative patterns of thinking*. Anything can send Alex's thought in a different direction, bringing back memories of other events and situations. When he 'comes back' from his detour the conversation has gone much further and he looks for some clues to fit in. Lisa's talk about a Pekinese puppy triggered the memory of the only Pekinese Alex knows – his grandmother's pet – Umka. During the last visit Umka jumped at the boy and he knocked down Granny's teapot. When Alex was back in the conversation with his apologies for breaking the teapot, Lisa was talking about other pets in her friend's family: 'two cats, too'. Far away from the topic of the conversation, Alex promptly did the sum – two plus two – he loves mathematics! And when Lisa mentioned Polly, for Alex it's out of the context of dogs and cats. It triggered the song in his head, that leads to the topic of 'tea' which he never drinks, that reminded him of his favourite drink – Coca-Cola, which brought the memory of his birthday celebration, which leads to something else again.

Last but not least: on the cognitive level autistic humans may experience difficulty when they want to stop thinking about something. On the perceptual level it is difficult to 'stop feeling' something, or 'sticky nails' in Alex's interpretation, when feeling lasts longer, sometimes much longer, than the real sensation. Thoughts can also be 'sticky'. Some autistic humans cannot stop thinking 'obsessive thoughts'. It may bring real frustration. It may cause not only mental exhaustion, but physical tiredness as well. For example, if the child thinks in 'kinaesthetic', the thoughts about climbing the tree are felt as real movements, so by the end of the hour this child may be fed up with mental climbing, but unable to stop it. What would his carers see? Challenging behaviours, of course. Tantrums 'out of the blue'. But are they out of the blue? They are out of the darkness – the inability of the child's carers to understand what is going on.

Next time you see an autistic child sitting in the corner, 'doing nothing', don't be fooled – the child is thinking!

CHAPTER 7

What is so Special about Special Abilities?

When humans talk about special abilities they mean something that they themselves cannot do. Those with extra-special abilities are called geniuses. On the other paw, people who cannot do what the majority can are labelled, at best, learning disabled, or, at worst, retarded. Thus the measuring stick for any skill is divided into several sections: geniuses (very few in number), above average (quite a few but still in a minority), average (or normal – the majority) and retarded. The question is, what if HSs cannot *see* special abilities, or they don't even know they exist? Where does the person with 'invisible' abilities end up? Bearing this in mind, is it a wonder that HSs assumed that animals were inferior to them? In fact, animals are smarter than humans think they are. Actually, HSs haven't got a clue of what animals can do. There are some animals who, like some humans, have a form of genius. Their talents are so extraordinary that no HSs could equal them, even with a lot of work and practice.[1] In her book Temple Grandin writes about feats of extreme memory and extreme perception in animals – something that most humans cannot do.[1] However, for animals exhibiting these abilities, their talents are not special; they are normal. To be logical, from the point of view of nHSs, humans must look retarded because they cannot do what an average representative of the animal kingdom can (see nHS IQ test, pp.36–37).

I've always wondered, however, is the 'extreme perception' about acuteness of the senses or something else? Some HSs call it a sixth sense. Personally I don't like this term. It's not because I disagree that the phenomenon it labels exists, but rather that it's an illogical label. Why is it a sixth sense? (Oh, sometimes HSs talk about a seventh sense as well.) As far as I and every kitten know humans have seven senses! Shouldn't it be called an 'eighth sense'? A few (more logical) HSs call it an extra sense. The second question to answer is: What is 'an extra sense'? The answer depends on the views of those who give it. Some HSs (also known as 'sceptics') define it as 'something that doesn't exist' or 'something that exists only in fiction'. Others (who are more cautious and don't want to deny something just because they don't fully understand it) describe the extra sense as 'a sensation of knowing something by instinct/intuition'. Another term used by the general public is 'a gut feeling' – a special kind of intuition.

A psychologist, Dr Ronald Rensink, conducted several tests on volunteers to prove that 'gut feeling', or 'mindsight', is real and some humans do possess it. His team showed the volunteers a series of pairs of pictures on a computer screen. Each image was shown for about a quarter of a second and followed by a brief blank grey screen. Some of the pictures were exactly the same throughout the trial, while others were slightly changed. A third of the volunteers reported feeling that images were alternated before they could identify what the change was. In control trials (images without changes), the same individuals were confident that there were no alterations whatsoever.[2] Dr Rensink clarifies that mindsight is not only about vision but may be about other senses too, for example, hearing – when you know someone is behind you, even when you cannot see them. In my opinion, both 'gut feeling' and 'mindsight' are inadequate descriptions because it is notnecessarily about proprioception or vision. The 'extra sense' is, in fact, not an additional sense some species (both human and proper animals) possess, but rather extra ability to sense the environment – extreme perception. Another study, by Dr Rollin McCraty, attempted to measure this elusive (sixth/seventh/eighth? – in short, extra) sense, or intuition. The volunteers were shown a series of images, most of them peaceful and calming, but they were interspersed with some shocking photos of car crashes or snakes ready to strike. The volunteers' hands were connected to the machine that monitored their heartbeats and sweat secretion. Between five and seven seconds before they saw a shocking image the equipment showed the increased heartbeat and the sweat level, indicating a subconscious fear response.[3]

Is this 'extra sense' the same as telepathy? HSs define telepathy as the supposed communication of thoughts or ideas other than by the known senses. I wouldn't mix the two. Extra ability to sense something because your senses are very acute is one thing; 'sensing the thoughts' and 'feeling what is about to happen' are quite another.

Animal lovers believe that their pets have astonishing abilities to perceive what is going on in the world, and explain them as extrasensory perception. Temple Grandin, however, refutes these views and accounts for animals' incredible perception as 'having a supersensitive apparatus'.[4] As an example, she gives several possible 'sensory cues' that her friend's cat could 'read' to announce her owner's arrival home at least five minutes before it actually happened. I can add more examples of extraordinary abilities that seem to rely on acute senses. Dogs may be able to 'smell' cancer. Cancer cells are believed to produce organic chemicals with distinctive ordours that dogs can smell. Some dogs can predict epileptic seizures and even protect their humans from injury. They learn to respond with 'first aid' behaviour after witnessing just one seizure.[5]

From my feline perspective, however, there are cases that cannot be accounted for by just super-acute senses; there is something else involved, something that HSs don't know yet. Oh, well... One thing is to say, 'I can't explain it because I don't know' and the other is to say, 'It doesn't exist because I don't know it.' Which one would you choose?

Another special 'sense-based' ability (often called condition) is *synaesthesia*, or cross-sensory perception. Both non-autistic and autistic HSs may have it.

> *Synaesthesia*: the ability to perceive stimulation of one sense via a different sensory modality. For example, I see 'red' when I hear dogs barking.

To translate it into plain English: if you answer 'yes' to one of the following questions you have synaesthesia:

- Can you see sounds?
- Can you smell colours?
- Can you taste shapes?
- Can you feel sounds on your skin?

Some humans may forget the name of the person they know but remember the colour, or taste, or even temperature of the word. There are very strange cases, where the spelling affects the taste, for example, 'Lori' tastes like a pencil eraser, but 'Lauri' tastes lemony.[6]

Synaesthesia may be of two types:

- *Two-sensory synaesthesia*: when two senses are involved, and stimulation of one modality triggers the perception in a second modality (in the absence of direct impact through the second sense).

- *Multiple sensory synaesthesia*: when more than two senses are involved.[7]

Synaesthesia is not specific to autism, but there are many parallels which are very telling. For example, humans with synaesthesia (like those with autism) have very good memory (due to the parallel sensations), but uneven cognitive skills. They are reported to prefer order, neatness, symmetry and balance; and they are more prone to unusual experiences such as déjà vu and clairvoyance.[6]

There is a very interesting hypothesis about the origin of synaesthesia (called the neonatal synaesthesia hypothesis) proposed by Maurer.[8] All human babies experience undifferentiated sensory input, when all senses are mixed up, probably up to four to six months of age. Non-human babies (including feline ones) seem to have similar transient connections between visual, auditory, somatosensory and motorcortex.[9] I cannot say it with certainty – I was too young to remember my first weeks' experiences. If the neonatal synaesthesia theory is correct, then synaesthesia is a normal phase of development. In this case, adult synaesthesia, as was suggested by Baron-Cohen and colleagues, might represent a breakdown in the process of differentiation of the senses.[10]

There are quite a few autistic humans who have synaesthesia as well. It is not easily detected because many autistic HSs with synaesthesia don't realise that other humans cannot, say, hear sounds while seeing colours. For them, it's a normal way to perceive the world. Besides, even very articulate adults with autism find it difficult to express their experiences because they are so different from the 'norm'. And of course, unappreciated... I know two autistic humans with synaesthesia. The first one is our Alex, who sees not only colours in response to sounds, but also words (yes, words) when he hears them. If he sees the 'wrong word' (or as he says his 'eyes see the wrong word') we are all in trouble. His panic attack is not far away, and the consequences may be unpredictable. The second autistic human with synaesthesia I know is Miss Ponytail. She *feels* sounds on her skin. Some sounds produce very pleasant tactile sensations, others are painful and 'disgusting' (her word). The worst is whistling: it feels like tearing her skin raw. Knowing Miss Ponytail as well as I do, I can imagine why she was banned from certain buses: some humans were whistling and she promptly asked them to shut up. The rest is history.

Temple Grandin compares animals with extreme talents to autistic savants.[1] Savant syndrome is thought to be a rare but extraordinary condition in which persons with serious mental disabilities have some 'island of genius' which stands in a marked contrast to things they cannot do. Only 10 per cent of autistic humans are said to have savant skills. Areas of skills traditionally attributed to savants are: musical and artistic ability, an exceptional ability to remember, spell and pronounce words, mathematical abilities, calendar calculating, geographical ability (reading maps, remembering directions, locating places), mechanical skills (taking apart and putting together complex mechanical and electrical equipment), a remarkable ability to balance things, spatial skills (the ability to estimate the size or distance of objects with great accuracy) and outstanding knowledge in specific fields (such as statistics, history, navigation).

Some savants may have a single special skill; others have several. Strangely enough, these extraordinary capabilities are often seen as a sign of dysfunction. Why can't we assume that as different cognitive mechanisms are involved in savant syndrome, these abilities become dysfunctional only in the environment that operates using different forms of processing and expressing information?

Inspired by the research of savants' abilities I've conducted my own. These are the conclusions I've come up with. The lists of savant abilities presented in different published papers are incomplete, because there are many abilities that are 'invisible' for 'normal' HSs. Humans can see or hear and appreciate only something spectacular: drawings that they could never do even with years of training; absolute musical pitch that is so rare in the 'normal' population; and so on. No wonder the film 'Rain Man' became so popular in the past and... earns a lot of loathing now. Humans were intrigued that a disabled person could do things they were unable to perform. Raymond's calendar calculation abilities were amazing. Not to mention his ability to remember the cards and win thousands of dollars in the Las Vegas casino. Now many autistic humans don't like the fictional character Raymond Babbitt – an autistic savant – because they say he misrepresents autism. They feel bitter that the general public expect spectacular abilities from *all* autistic individuals. Actually, they are wrong. Due to the differences in information processing and remarkable memory, *all* autistics can do something non-autistic humans cannot. The only differences between humans like Raymond and 'average autistics' are:

- autistic savants are not overwhelmed with the information flowing through their senses

- autistic savants can perform or reproduce via art the information they have stored in their memory.

Autistic non-savants have the same capacity to memorise things but they may be easily overwhelmed with the information and/or cannot reproduce it in a spectacular way.

Some very special abilities are 'invisible' to non-autistic humans because they cannot imagine them. Those HSs and nHSs who have spent at least some time with an autistic person would notice a very important characteristic of autism: fascination with sensory stimuli. The sources of fascination are very individual. One and the same stimulus can cause disturbance (when it is too 'sharp') and fascination to different children. This is just a surface behaviour, and most humans stop at this point. The 'normal' interpretation is: 'The child is staring at the leaf, withdrawn in his own world. We have to make him pay attention to normal activities.' What 'normal' humans cannot see, however, is that the child is absorbed with the brilliance of the colour and the perfect proportions of intrinsic patterns formed by the 'veins' of this ideal piece of nature. This ability to greatly appreciate colour, sound, texture, smell or taste, to resonate with the stimulus, to *feel* it is very typical for many humans on the autism spectrum. But this special talent turns out to be useless in the world that is blind, deaf and dumb to the real physical environment, to the beauty of nature and amazing harmony of sights, sounds and texture. It is sad, really. Potentially all humans have remarkable abilities because they are already there, inside their brains.[1] The trick is how to get access to these capabilities. Savants can do it easily. 'Normal' HSs seem to have problems – or shall I meow 'learning difficulties'?

This brings us to the subject of intelligence and the object of measuring it: the IQ test. What is intelligence? As I've found out, nobody knows the answer. There are so many vague definitions that can be summarised as: 'Intelligence is what we measure with intelligence tests.' My definition is also a bit vague, but it's a start.

> *Intelligence*: the understanding of the world, and the ability to think about it and act on it.

> *IQ tests*: tests designed to measure intelligence.

About 70 per cent of autistic humans are considered to be intellectually disabled. This claim is based on the results of standard IQ tests. The key word here is 'standard': the IQ tests are designed to determine whether a person is developing within 'normal' range or is 'slow' or 'stuck' in his or her development. However, as autistic humans follow a different path in their development, they are not 'less developed versions' of non-autistic humans but rather humans who have developed, sometimes substantially, along a very different track from non-autistic HSs, while acquiring a whole range of adaptations, compensations and strategies on the way. Their abilities, while 'invisible', may be so unusual that no existing test can measure them. The problem with standard IQ tests is, they do *not* identify 'autistic intelligence'. This is very unfortunate, because if HSs had the knowledge of the 'inner abilities' and mechanisms autistic humans have acquired they could better teach autistic persons to function in the non-autistic world and, consequently, they could score a higher IQ.[11]

What do humans really measure with IQ tests if they do not take into account perceptual and cognitive differences? No wonder there are so many HSs with labels of 'intellectually disabled' or 'retarded'. If somebody behaves differently from the 'norm' humans are quick to doubt the person's intelligence. The same is true about humans' interpretation of animals' behaviour and intelligence: if an animal resembles humans or acts like one, humans see this animal as more intelligent. The appearances, however, may be deceptive. Every animal is as clever as it needs to be. Every animal has skills that are necessary for its functioning.[12]

And here we have another problem. Human 'environment is built to the specifications and limitations of a normal human perceptual system'[13] that may be not very suitable for autistic HSs. What's to be done? Some very one-sided humans would say, 'They [autistics] are in a minority. Let them adjust to our world.' Some 'other-sided' humans would cry out, 'Society must accommodate and adjust the environment to the needs of autistic humans! They have the right to be who they are!' Who is right? Both and neither. The fact of the matter is, different autistic humans have different needs, sometimes contradictory to each other. For example, one person may love the sound of running water and another would find it nearly impossible to tolerate. How can you accommodate these two in one and the same environment? Or take another case. Our Alex hates the sound of babies crying – it hurts his ears. Does this mean that humans have to ban babies from all public places in case Alex wants to go there? (OK, personally, I have succeeded in making *my* demands matter. But my case is an exception. My mates have adjusted both the physical and emotional environment to *my* very special needs. I meow once, and they jump; I meow twice, and they jump two times; I meow three times, and… I fly out of the premises. The speed they send me out of the house is a bit fast for my liking, but otherwise it's good for my health – fresh air, you know.)

Anyway, isn't it more fair and beneficial for everybody to approach the problem from two different directions? One side would try to take into account different ways of functioning and adjust the environment to make it easier for autistic HSs to access. For example, fluorescent lights are not a necessity, or non-autistic humans could teach their non-autistic offspring good manners and supervise them in public places. The other side could seek and get help to overcome treatable difficulties (for example, hypersensitivities can be addressed via different exercises, tinted glasses, earplugs and so on). Besides, both sides have to educate themselves about differences and learn to respect each other.

We all have different abilities. This is true for both human animals and non-human animals. Some can do certain things much better than others, but be useless in other areas. Why can't all appreciate each other for what they can do well, and help with areas they struggle with?

CHAPTER 8

Language and Communication: Let's Talk about Talking

Language and communication impairments are said to be essential characteristics of autism. Of course, I disagree. Not about the fact that language and communication characteristics are different in autism (I agree with that, no problem), but that they are 'impaired'. Even from my limited experience of living with an autistic individual and observing his autistic friends, I can state with all confidence that autistic humans are not 'communicatively *impaired*' – they do communicate; they are communicating all the time. They just speak a different language and have their own communication systems.

The same erroneous assumption was made about animals. Till recently, some researchers believed that animal communication was 'mechanical', and animal languages were primitive, and indeed couldn't be called languages at all. But hold on a minute. What is communication?

Communication: transmission of information between individuals.

Like humans, animals have their own societies, with quite a complex social structure. It would be impossible to live in a (human or non-human) society without the ability to communicate, negotiate and let one's needs be known. Each species uses their own language. For example, ants use a highly sophisticated communication system – based on 'chemical language' – to send 'messages' to one another. They lay a chemical trail to inform other members of their community where food can be found or, if there is a danger, their body produces chemicals containing a different message: 'Be ready for an attack from foes.'

Or take us cats, for example. We do communicate, but our communication methods are very different from humans. This doesn't give HSs the right to deny our ability to receive and transmit information. Felinologically speaking, using our methods we get much more information from our communicative partner in seconds, while it may take humans months to know the person they have befriended. For example, when I encounter a cat whom I've never met before, I sniff to receive chemical information about his status, age, family background, where he comes from, the meal he has had recently, and many other things I'm interested in. How long would it take a human female to learn all this information about her date? And if he is not quite honest with her, how long will it take her to check all the facts he has provided? Sometimes years! In my case, the information I get is accurate and 'delivered' in seconds. Are you interested? Do you want to learn feline communication – 'sniff-code'? Well… I'm not sure if you really want to know which part of the body you have to sniff in order to get the most complete information about the identity of your partner. So let's leave it at that.

Cats also use tactile contact (combined with scent) to send messages. There are scent glands all over my body, especially on the cheeks, beneath the chin, around the mouth, the forehead, the tail and between the toes. To send my message I rub against the person to leave my 'smelly text' for him or her to interpret. When I communicate with my kin, it's not a problem. But I've tried many a time to make my housemates receive SMSs. Alas, they cannot read my sophisticated messages. I've also tried body language with them. When I want to show that I'll fight for my rights, I do my best to look bigger than I am to frighten my opponent away. I arch my back as high as I can, and fluff my fur up. My message is clear: 'Do you dare argue with me now?' If I opt not to fight, I use a different body posture. For example, I don't really like to argue with Polly since she is my friend and besides she is much bigger than I am. In this case, I lower my body to the ground with my ears down and flat to look smaller than I am: 'Let's forget our argument. Look, I'm so small and cute!' And when I'm in my social mood I perform my 'social roll', lying down to expose my tummy: 'Let's be friends and play.' My other tool of communication is my 'talkative tail'. When I'm going on business my tail's position is horizontal: 'I'm busy. Don't interrupt me. I know what I'm doing.' If I meet a friend (either another cat or a human) I greet him or her with my tail high and upright, with a slight curve of its tip forward. If I meet someone unfriendly and the negotiations fail I put my tail down to get it out of the way and prepare to fight. But if you see my tail twitching, it means I'm still considering if the attack is imminent, and you have a few seconds to ask for a truce.

Humans pay too much attention to facial expressions at the cost of much more expressive 'ear language'. For example, when I'm relaxed (but alert) I put my ears forward and erect. If I'm angry or frightened but don't want to show it, I turn my ears backward and simultaneously open my mouth to show my teeth: 'Don't you want to reconsider your position towards me?' As for eye contact that is so important for HSs, in feline society it's the opposite: it's not polite to stare. Some HSs are surprised that cat lovers never get attention from a cat when they visit their friend living with a feline companion. All their 'pussy-pussy's are ignored. But if someone who doesn't like cats (or even actively dislikes them) is in the same room, the cat would do everything to jump on his or her lap. The former representative of the humankind is seen by the cat as impolite or even rude, while the latter is not staring at the cat, meaning it's safe to be with this person. On the other paw, blinking or narrowing eyes is the cat's very polite way to show friendliness.

We cats create our notice boards as well, where we leave messages for those who are literate in felinese. When I scratch furniture, carpet or trees, I leave eloquent texts about my present needs and interests. These messages involve several sensory channels – visual and smell ones. Alas, humans cannot read them, and (what is even worse) try to stop my writing exercises with the very poor excuse of protecting the furniture. I have tried a stronger language – urine and faeces messages in the living room. The illiterate lot took them as an insult! Where is the logic in this interpretation? So I had to find a solution. Like any other animals who've been in contact with humans for some time, we learn how to initiate and sustain a conversation with HSs. From my experience, humans react better to sound than smell and body language. I meow when I want their attention. Sometimes we have to become very vocal to make our needs met and our feelings known. There still might be misunderstanding, but only because humans and felines speak different languages!

Establishing communication and understanding between any two creatures with different experiences and perceptions involves developing a common language.

> *Language*: typically defined as a system of symbols and methods of combination of these symbols that serves as a means of communication and formulating and expressing thoughts.

Most HSs assume that 'signs' in this definition always mean words. However, though conventional, verbal words are not the only signs that satisfy the criteria of language. It is logical therefore to distinguish two types of languages: verbal (consisting of words) and non-verbal (consisting of non-verbal symbols).[1] Human animals are strange creatures. They assume that if non-human animals cannot talk their language, they have no language at all. They try to find out which animals can *learn* human language (the only language possible from some HSs's perspective) and which are 'hopeless'. They design training procedures, conduct their experiments and publish the results in peer-reviewed journals. No one, to my knowledge, has done any research yet about whether humans can *learn* animal languages, or whether they are hopeless. I'd like to make a statement. Before we start our exploration of autistic communication and languages, I'd like to leave a coded (non-smelly) message for those who enjoy challenges.[2]

At this stage of evolution, 3–8–5–13
2–15–12–19–8–5 21–26–14–1–25–21
12–25–21–4–5–25, 20–5–13 2–15–12–19–8–5
20–19–5–14–25–21
15–4–9–14–15–3–8–5–19–20–22–15.

Traditionally, HSs see verbal language as a key prognostic factor in autism, and the level of language and communicative competence achieved by a person as a measure of the outcome. However, even those with a very good structural language ability are said to be communicatively impaired in autism. Now we know for sure they all communicate; it's those around them who don't recognise their attempts to transmit information. Autistic HSs do not lack the desire to talk to others but rather use unconventional means of communication – the language that non-autistic HSs do not share with them. As their languages are so different, they have difficulty in using any conventional system in all but the most basic ways. And, of course, in order to communicate successfully, non-autistic and autistic humans need shared experiences. As autistic and non-autistic HSs process information differently, they do not share the experiences of one and the same situation. Isn't it any wonder that both parties find the interaction difficult? For example, many autistic individuals find it strange that if there are a few humans present one is expected to talk about anything, even if they have nothing in common. It is being polite for the sake of politeness. However, some HSs do not need 'empty' social contact; they may be bored but they do not feel lonely. Isn't it more logical to communicate only with those who are interested in you as a person? Or, what is the point of smiling and being polite if you don't like the person? Isn't it better just to ignore that person or leave? Or to say 'I'm fine' when you are not? Should you lie to 'get it right'?[3] Miss Ponytail confessed once that she hated (and tried to avoid) situations where she was forced to conduct an 'empty conversation' – talking about nothing with humans who are not interested in her but keep firing questions without listening to her answers. I remember the first time I met her, when she came to Mother to discuss possible strategies to cope with 'normal' HSs at her workplace. It was a quiet afternoon and I was at the passive stage of my research, i.e. sleeping on the settee while my brain was registering what was going on. For the first ten minutes there seemed to be nothing of value for either my security or research, when suddenly my attention was grasped by the question: 'Who do you think are the most talkative people in the world?', which our friend with Asperger syndrome, seemingly shattered and upset, asked the hosts. Both Mother and Dad looked at each other and made a weak attempt to give the right answer – 'Newsreaders?'

'No! Hairdressers. I hate to have my hair done because they just don't shut up! Why do they want to know about me, my family, where I go on my holidays, what I think about the weather and what I did last weekend? It's none of their business! OK, it was a mistake to tell them this... Do you know any hairdresser in your area I could try next?'

'I go to the salon across the road. They are not very expensive and...'

The information Mother provided turned out to be useless:

'No good. I was banned from there last year. Oh, well. I'll have to wear a ponytail all my life.' Since that day she's been known as Miss Ponytail.

Autistic children, like non-autistic ones, learn through interactions with the world, but this interaction is qualitatively different. They learn their language(s) through interaction with objects and other humans on the sensory level. That is why their 'words' have nothing to do with the conventional names for things and events that non-autistic HSs use to describe the function of these things and events. Their 'words' are 'sensory templates': if something 'feels' the same they know what to do about it; if the 'feeling' is a little bit different they do not understand this 'word' and may be confused. Their 'words' are literal (stored sensations produced by objects through interaction) and they name them accordingly. One sense (sometimes several) becomes dominant for storing memories, developing 'language', and constructing thoughts. There are several 'sensory-based languages':

- *Visual language:* children use visual images.

- *Tactile language:* children 'speaking' tactile language recognise things by touching them, feeling textures and surfaces with their hands, bare feet, or their cheeks. Through touch they get the information about the size and form of things, but not about their function or purpose. They store the information for later reference and may find similar objects (for example, a plastic cup and a glass cup) to be completely different 'words' in their vocabulary because they 'feel' different.

- *Kinaesthetic language*: children learn about things through the physical movements of their body. Each thing or event is identified by a certain pattern of body movements. They know places and distances by the amount and pattern of the movement of the body.

- *Auditory language*: children remember objects and events by 'sound pictures'. If the object is 'silent', they may tap it to recognise it by the sound it produces.

- *Smell language*: objects and other humans are identified by smell.

- *Taste language*: children lick objects to feel the taste they give on the tongue.[1]

No wonder spoken words are often perceived as mere sounds. How can you see, hear or feel me, for example, in a verbal frame of CAT? The best interpreter I'm aware of, from verbal to sensory words, is Donna Williams who described her sensory vocabulary in her (very insightful and intelligent) books. When a child, Donna had two 'sensory words' for my kin: one was 'foosh', defined by the sound she heard when stroking the fur of the cat; the other was 'brook' defined by the noise we cats produce when humans stroke us.[4]

Young autistic children may not recognise an object by its verbal name. However, they may identify it by the sound it produces, or smell, or feel in the hand. Each child may use one or several 'languages' to make sense about the world. Eventually, with the humans around them using the same communication system as the child, the child learns to connect the 'auditory envelope' with the inner images in his or her preferred sensory modality. Before autistic children can learn a 'foreign language' the carers have to learn the language of their child in order to develop some common means of communication. It also enables them to 'interpret' the child's messages. The trick is to find out what non-verbal language each particular autistic child speaks. (Didn't I tell you that whatever autism is, it is never boring?)

Sometimes parents of newly diagnosed children think that as soon as their child starts talking all the problems will be behind them. However, this is not the case in autism. When the child starts to talk, his or her speech is characterised with specific 'autistic' features.

After my first experiment of social interaction (described in Chapter 3) I (Dasha, the researcher) gave myself (but in the capacity of Dasha, the student) an assignment to investigate the features of autistic verbal language. (One day I hope I'll complete my PhD on the subject of autism.) I'm proud to present my first collection of 'research essays' under the title *Peculiarities of Verbal Language in Autism.*

Echolalia

The first, most visible (or to be more exact – audible) sign of 'autistic verbal language' is echolalia.

> *Echolalia:* the parrot-like repetition of another person's spoken words. There are usually two distinguishable

types of echolalia: *immediate echolalia* (or repetition of words and phrases just heard), e.g. Mother: 'Do you want an ice-cream?' Child: 'You want an ice-cream'; and *delayed echolalia* (or repetition of words and phrases heard in the past), e.g. when having a meal, the child announces, 'May the Force be with you!'

As far as I know, many non-autistic children use echolalia as a language-learning strategy when they start talking, but this is a short phase which lasts until they learn to change the patterns of words and sentences. In autism echolalia lasts much longer, or even remains the only verbal means of expression a person possesses. Echolalia in autism is one of the features of the Gestalt strategy of language acquisition, when a child uses whole chunks of verbal utterances as single 'words'.[5] It may be both communicative and non-communicative. In the case of non-communicative echolalia, words and phrases are 'sensory toys' to play with: a lot of autistic humans will produce sounds, words or phrases to themselves, just in order to get some auditory or tactile pleasure. Alex, for instance, loves to play with 'funny words', repeating them again and again. He may be very creative, making words sound funny by changing one letter in them: 'pound' becomes 'vound', 'kitchen' becomes 'mitchen' and 'boy' becomes 'poy'.

In many cases, however, echolalia is *communicative*, and can serve several functions:

- It can mean 'I don't understand'. It increases when children are confused and cannot work out what is going on around them. They know some sort of response is expected from them, but what were they asked? 'Dontyourepeateverythingivesaid!' – 'Dontyourepeateverythingivesaid.'

- Echolalia can be a means to 'win time' (in the case of delayed processing) or to 'get the meaning' from what has been said as some autistic HSs understand speech better if they repeat the message. Immediate echolalia in this case is a strategy to 'translate' verbal words into meaningful inner language.

- Echolalia may be interpreted as a request. When echolalia is the only means of communication at the child's disposal, he would repeat the question he was asked, when he wants to get this item. For instance, when a child wants a biscuit he says: 'Do you want a biscuit?' It's very clever, really, to use the phrase the child has heard when he was offered a treat, when the child wants a biscuit.

Demanding the same verbal scenario

Autistic children often demand that people say exactly the same words they have used in a similar situation. Otherwise the situation is incomplete (Gestalt is different) and they do not know how to respond or what to do next. I have been watching all sorts of 'performances' for years: 'matinees' (in the morning), 'dress rehearsals' (at lunchtime) and 'open nights' (bedtime). In the beginning (a few years ago) all the 'actors' (members of the family) had to learn their lines by heart and be very careful to avoid replacing one word for the other in the scripts. Alex would demand a perfect perfor-mance, or... the actors didn't want the 'or' option. Every morning, Mother would say, 'Good morning, Alex, it's time to get up.' Alex would reply, 'I don't want to get up.' Mother: 'If you don't want to go to school, stay in bed.' Alex: 'I want to get up.' Mother: 'Get up, then.' Once, about three years ago, Mother forgot to say 'then'. She was reminded of the importance of knowing her lines by Alex's (very loud) reaction and response…from the neighbours who rushed into their house thinking their friends had some serious trouble. Lunchtime performances and open night plays were even more sophisticated. It wasn't enough just to say your lines, but they had to be said with the same intonation and from the same place 'on the stage'. With time (and a lot of explanation and reassurance), however, Alex has become more flexible and is quite happy to prompt when someone in the cast has forgotten their lines: 'Say,…'. If the cast display selective deafness he performs for all the play characters, for example: 'I'm going to bed – Yes, it's time – Will you kiss me goodnight – Of course I will.'

Affirmation by repetition

'Yes' is often a difficult word for autistic children to use and understand. It takes them longer to master it, and for years they may repeat the sentence when they mean 'yes'. During one of my passive research activities (I mean sleeping) the explanation came to me unexpectedly. Suddenly it became clear why they do it: you cannot sensorily define 'yes'; you cannot see it, or hear it, or feel it on your skin and it doesn't smell. How can you translate it into a comprehensible image? To work around this difficulty, the child who wants to respond affirmatively will repeat the question he or she was asked. If the child is asked whether he or she wants an ice-cream, the response may be 'Do you want an ice-cream?', meaning 'Yes, I do,' or 'Of course I do!'

Extreme literalness

The main (and very logical) feature in autistic language, however, is their extreme literalness. One verbal word has only one 'inner image' – something the child can refer to in his or her 'mental vocabulary'. Some autistic children seem to have difficulty accepting synonyms. I share their frustration. How can two or even more words refer to one and the same thing? Alex was completely confused when a visitor, collecting donations for charity, asked him whether she could sit with him on the sofa. 'But we have no sofa!' said Alex who was sitting on the *settee.* The visitor took it as an offence and complained to Mother that the boy was making fun of her. It was a big mistake. Huge! She thought that Mother would discipline her son (who hadn't done anything wrong, by the way). The visitor was 'disciplined' instead; Mother gave her an hour and a half lecture on autism (and a cup of tea to go with it). Actually, the 'punishment' turned into 'reward'. The lady became very interested in the subject and asked many questions. She happened to know a family with an autistic child and Mother's explanations helped her interpret some of his 'insulting' behaviours, such as his comments on her being 'very old and wrinkled'.

Alex's ability to read brings some problems as well. It is hard for him to understand that words that have the same pronunciation may have different spellings, or those words that are spelled differently can sound the same, or the words do not mean what they mean. For example, the family went shopping to buy some food for a barbecue. They were all in a very good mood when they left. The mood they had when they came back was a different matter. I knew what had happened from a telephone conversation (Mother told the story to her friend). In the shop there was a huge display of tins and cans with a big advertising notice on the top of the shelf: 'Grab and Go!' So Alex did just that – he grabbed the tin of hot dogs and went. Unfortunately, the security guard was not impressed with Alex's compliance to do what he was told.

It's a pity that many humans who are in contact with autistic HSs often forget about their literalness, and when unexpected outcomes emerge they put all the blame on the autistic humans being difficult. For example, Miss Ponytail has found herself in trouble many times just because she trusted her acquaintances. Once she was visiting her colleague who was on sick leave and the latter said, 'It's been very kind of you to come to see me. Pop in any time you are in the neighbourhood.' A couple of days later Miss Ponytail did just that (popped in when she was in the neighbourhood) but her colleague refused to open the door and called the police. The colleague should have been more specific and told Miss Ponytail that she didn't mean the time between midnight and 7 am (when Miss Ponytail was returning from her shift at work). So whose fault was it that Miss Ponytail had to explain her behaviour at the police station and got a bad reputation among the neighbours?

Pronoun reversal

All children go through a stage when they experience difficulty in using pronouns, especially 'I/me' and 'you'. Non-autistic children soon overcome this difficulty by practising the use of appropriate forms in pretend play with social roles. For children with autism the confusion over the correct use of the pronouns is quite profound and even autistic adults may have problems with it. They prefer to use their proper names to refer to themselves or to others. Again, it's very logical: one word stands for one object. In the case of pronouns (and other deictic words, for example, 'here–there', 'this–that'), the words seem to jump from one person or one place to the other all the time. For instance, Mother was 'I' five minutes ago when she talked about her shopping trip, but then Father asked her about the traffic, and she became 'you'. It is confusing for autistic children, as they have difficulty in understanding that one and the same thing, person or place can have several 'names' attached to them.

> *Deictic words*: words that 'cannot stay still'; they jump from one object or place to the other, depending where the person who uses them stands. For example, 'here–there': what is 'here' for you, is 'there' for someone at the other end of the room; 'this–that': you are reading 'this' book, but it suddenly becomes 'that' book for someone who is in the kitchen.

There are other difficult words to understand because they 'move' in time. For instance, how on earth can 'today' become 'yesterday' tomorrow?

Metaphorical language

To autistic humans certain words may have some private meanings different from their common definitions. Their 'metaphorical words' do make sense if you know their origin. For example, Alex calls small amounts of things 'sip it!', since that was his mother's advice not to gulp the glass of water in one go. Lacking the information about the origin of this meaning, many humans were confused when he commented 'There are "sip it" sweets left. We have to buy more.'

Repetitive questioning

Autistic children often ask the same questions repetitively (especially when they are anxious and confused). Although they know the answer they want to hear it again. The problem is that the answer must always be the same, and if their 'communicative partner' does not provide the 'right' answer a tantrum may follow. A child repeats the same question not for the sake of getting information, but to maintain a predictable reaction, to be reassured everything is going fine.

~~~

These and other 'autistic language peculiarities' are perfectly logical if their perceptual, cognitive and language processes are taken into account. The usefulness of verbal language for an autistic child will depend on the degree to which the child shares meaning of the verbal words with humans from whom he or she learns the language. If the carers and teachers introduce communication systems matching the child's inner (internal) language, it will help the child 'translate' from external to internal 'code'. If they use one system (for example, pictures) for all children in the classroom, for some it might work, and for others it might not. What I've noticed during my encounters with autistic humans is that they often try to teach non-autistics how to communicate with them. It is not their fault that non-autistic HSs do not see the very subtle clues they give them.

CHAPTER 9

Emotions:
Love Me?
Love Me Not?

And here we come to empathy and emotions. There is a lot of talk about emotions in relation to animals and humans. However, there is no universal agreement about what emotions are. Some think of emotions as feelings, while others prefer to distinguish between these two concepts. I belong to the latter group. Maybe it is because English is my second language and I want to understand the differences between the words in order to grasp the actual meanings of different acoustic and written representations, 'enveloping' these meanings. So here goes:

Feelings: physical sensations that can be *somatic* and *affective*. *Somatic* experiences are feelings of the body, for example, muscle tension, tiredness, headache, chest pain, goose bumps, etc. *Affective* experiences are feelings of the soul, for example, emptiness, panic, etc.

Emotions: interpretations of feelings when both somatic and affective feelings are experienced as a kind of sensory–perceptual input with cognitive explanation and conscious plan of action.

Shweder defines emotions as complex narrative structures that give shape and meaning to somatic and affective experiences.[1] First you *feel* something, then you interpret what it is (by giving the name to the feeling), and then you act on it (or sometimes you act on it before you have time to interpret what you feel). To emotionalise one's feelings means to give a 'reading' to somatic and affective experiences. And it is not that simple! For example, you may feel sick, but does that mean that you have eaten something nasty or that you are in love? The somatic feeling may be the same – sickness – but its affective side is different.[2]

Traditionally, emotions are subdivided into primary (basic) and complex emotions. Basic emotions are simple emotions out of which all other complex emotions can be generated. These emotions include happiness, sadness, anger, fear and disgust. Complex emotions are ... well, complex. Carter gives an example of a complex emotion she defines as 'the pleasure-tinged-with-guilt-streaked-with-affection-and-irritation'.[3] Too much for me, I'm not going to dissect and analyse this 'emotional soup'. I prefer simple emotions, you know.

Do HSs and nHSs emotionalise, or 'read', their feelings the same way, i.e. do they have the same emotions? It turns out that animals have the same basic emotions as humans. This is true not only about mammals but also about birds and other animals. Even lizards and snakes share most emotions with humans.[4] Temple Grandin writes about the skink lizard in Australia and rattlesnake in the USA who are very good parents and protect their offspring from predators the same way a mammal or a human would. I personally love elephants. Maybe it is because of my attachment to Alex and his collection of toy elephants. These big, intelligent and beautiful creatures are very emotional too. When an elephant cries, the others comfort him. When members of the same family are reunited after a long period of separation, they go running to greet each other with the same affection as HSs would.[5]

Elephants' sense of compassion is as huge as their size! They comfort their youngsters when they feel fragile by putting their trunks on the baby-elephants' backs. They cover a dead body with their trunks, showing their grief.

Cats are very affectionate, though sometimes their humans do not see it. The most telling behaviour of feline love is kneading. What can be more meaningful and loving when I sit on the front or on the back of my human (who should be either in a horizontal or semi-horizontal position) kneading with my front paws, my claws in and out, suckling the fabric of whatever the human is wearing, purring my head off because it reminds me of my own mother and the security I felt with her? I'm not meowing that my HSs don't appreciate when I show my affection to them. They do. But what puzzles me completely is why Mother's appreciation depends on the clothes she wears during my 'session of affection'. If she has her jeans and an old jumper on, she is very responsive to my signs of love. Actually she purrs with me (her vocal cords are hopeless, though. The best she can do is 'yourethemostbeau-tifulcatdarling'.) However, when Mother changes into what she calls her 'socially presentable outfit', the more 'lovable' she looks, the less ready she is to appreciate my affection. Isn't it illogical? (I accepted long ago, as it is impossible for humans to know exactly what it is like to be a bat, or a cat, it is also impossible for a cat to know what it is like to be a human. We just have to keep trying to achieve some mutual understanding.)

Another behaviour which shows my ability to love my human family is to share my prey with them. Cats actually look after their housemates (not that some HSs appreciate the effort!). I don't contribute to our neighbours' meal, for example. I bring everything I catch to the very special HSs in my life. I wish them to show some respect for my way of looking after them.

Both behaviours – kneading and sharing – are examples of the cat's ability to love unconditionally. This means that, unlike many humans, we animals love not because of something but because we *love* special creatures in our life, sometimes *despite* their reluctance (or even active rejection) to accept it. It really doesn't matter to me how loud Mother screams when I bring my contribution to the kitchen or how high she jumps and balances on the surfaces of tables, chairs, the washing machine and once even the radiator. I'll keep doing it, because I love them.

A 'canine example' of unconditional love is that shown by Polly. It's funny, because both the females, Polly and the Woman (aka Wife of Polly's Man), love their Man very much, but they express it so differently. For example, the later he comes home from work, the happier Polly is to see him, whereas his Wife seems to have the opposite feeling. Why is she always angry when her Man is late? Well, it's difficult to understand humans. Temple Grandin points out that the main difference between animal emotions and human emotions is that animals don't have *mixed emotions* (for example, love–hate relationships with each other) the way most humans do.[4] That's why animals are loyal. If they love you, they love you no matter what. Temple Grandin shows in her book that autistic humans have mostly simple emotions too. Their feelings are direct and open: they either like you or they don't. It doesn't mean they can never experience mixed emotions, however. For example, the emotions of fear and curiosity can go together.

Panksepp believes that most species possess unique sensory perceptual inputs that lead to emotionality.[6] For example, for a rat to exhibit 'fearful' behaviours in response to the smell of me (or any other cat) requires no life experiences with cats.[7] Such behaviours are not acquired by learning. They are 'there' from the very beginning.[8] Emotions can begin so quickly that they can happen before the person is aware that they are happening.[9] Neither humans nor animals can decide something like 'OK, now I'm going to feel happy.' Emotions are happening to individuals, not chosen by them.

Kanner was the first to suggest that autistic children's primary deficit is their 'inability to relate themselves in the ordinary way to people and situations from the beginning of life'.[10] Though autism is more complicated than disturbances in affective contact, the problems with emotions do exist. This is my second collection of research essays: *Possible Difficulties with Emotions in Autism*.

Difficulty recognising emotions in others

This feature brings a lot of misunderstanding and 'miscommunication'. Strangely enough, HSs who are proudly claimed to be the only species on earth with 'proper' language (whatever 'proper language' means), opt to communicate emotions without it. They say, 'It's not what you say but how you say it' (or something along these lines). Communicating emotions seems to be idiosyncratic in the human population. They may say one thing, meaning completely the opposite. For example, when Alex (by accident) broke the vase that was Grandmother's present, his Dad reacted very strangely – he thanked the boy. Yes, he said, 'Thank you very much!' I couldn't believe my ears because I expected him to be upset. What happened next was even more odd. Alex, being polite, replied with 'You are welcome' and instead of admiring his son's good manners, Dad stamped his feet and started shouting something incomprehensible. Alex and myself were utterly confused – was he pleased or angry?

It appears that 90 per cent of emotions are communicated via facial expressions, tone of voice and body language, and only 10 per cent via words. Some autistic individuals find it difficult to 'read' facial expressions, intonation and body language because of their sensory perceptual differences and lack of shared experiences with non-autistic HSs. Some autistic humans, for example, cannot figure out what other humans mean when they pull faces. What is the point of curving, wrinkling up or just distorting different areas of the face? Others find it hard to interpret the tone of voice as 'emotionally coloured'.

Having meowed that, some autistic humans easily pick up the emotions of others and may be very distressed by the emotional behaviour of humans around them. Poor Mother can rarely afford to look angry or upset. Alex 'reads' her perfectly well; he 'resonates' with his mother's emotional state and experiences the same emotion inside him.

Difficulty in expressing emotions

Emotions can be expressed by facial expressions, vocalisation, posture and gesture. Autistic children may experience difficulties in expressing emotions that would be easily understandable by others. For example, in their facial expressions autistic children tend to show only the extremes of emotion, in ways that are considered by non-autistic humans inappropriate for their age and the social situation.[11] Some emotions may be expressed at full volume (especially frustration, anger, rage), and others 'silently'. When Alex can't unzip his coat (sometimes it does happen, but every time with a new coat because the old one becomes 'unusable' after each episode), not only his family know about his frustration (and anger directed at the coat) but probably some neighbours as well. Oh, and sometimes casualties include not only the coat but the furniture too. However, I do understand his mother's desire to buy a bottle of champagne and celebrate when Alex just touched her shoulder and rubbed his cheek against hers.

As the most loveable (and modest) creature in our neighbourhood, I can confirm that these expressions of love from Alex are priceless.

One of my favourite autistic authors, Jim Sinclair, wrote a very insightful article on this topic. He argues that no one ever bothered to explain to him that they expected to *see* feelings on his face, or that it confused them when Jim used words without corresponding expressions. How could he know this if nobody explained to him what the signals were or how to use them? He finally started learning to talk about emotions when he was 25. Jim's friend happened to be someone who talked a lot about her own feelings. She identified what each feeling was called, and where she felt it, and what her face and her body were doing about it, and what words described these emotions.[12] Jim's friend wasn't a professional but her 'approach' worked. In my humble opinion, good examples exist to be followed.

The ability to feel but difficulty in interpreting the feeling

Difficulty in understanding and expressing emotions does not mean that autistic HSs lack emotions. Some autistic humans *feel* all the emotions others feel, but can't interpret what they are feeling. Mother knows this simple truth and constantly teaches Alex to learn explicitly to recognise, label and understand the meaning of emotions and what to do about them. She teaches him that different emotions have different facial and bodily expressions. She follows Jim Sinclair's advice to explain some signals humans use to express their feelings and how others should respond when they notice these signals.[13] I love these sessions and always try to contribute to Mother's explanations pretending that I am a teacher's assistant. But of course (as usual) my humans do not appreciate it; we have trilogues instead of proper conversations. Once I did manage to intervene and attract their attention (when they were discussing 'happiness'). I purred so loudly that they both stopped at their tracks. And when I thought I had provided the best illustration of 'happiness', Alex asked, 'Why is Dasha always sad?'

OK, I admit I failed to express my feelings again, though Mother seemed to have some understanding.

'She is not sad now. She is happy.'

Alex didn't take it, 'But she never smiles. You've said, people smile when they are happy.'

'That's right. When people feel happy they smile. Cats are different, they do not smile, they purr...'

'So if Dasha purrs it means she is happy.'

I saw that Mother didn't want to confuse him, but she didn't want to lie to him, either.

'Not necessarily. Sometimes cats purr when they are in pain.'

Mother's love for the truth ended the lesson. Alex didn't want to hear any more.

'How am I supposed to understand it, if it means so many different things? It's illogical and confusing.'

He rushed out of the room and slammed the door behind him. Oh, well, he has expressed his anger very eloquently.

Another difficulty is that, as autistic humans have problems with abstract concepts, they can have problems with the *meaning* of emotional words. How could you describe in sensory language the meaning of 'fear', 'anger', 'love', 'kindness'? Miss Ponytail confessed to Mother that it took her 29 years to understand that the unpleasant feeling in her stomach was 'fear', and a terrifying feeling in her head meant 'panic'. Some other high-functioning autistic HSs use metaphors to explain their emotions, for example, 'explosion of gas' as 'anger'.

The combination of 'intellectual emotions' with 'emotional emotions'

Edgar Schneider, an adult human with Asperger syndrome, talks about being able to feel and appreciate intellectually great emotions through art, music, literature and other creative intellectual and aesthetic means. This is because through the arts, emotions are translated into sights, sounds, and words.[14] It doesn't mean, however, that he lacks all 'emotional emotions'. Emotions such as fear and anger (Schneider calls them 'survival' emotions) are very much present, but 'connective/intuitive' ones – the emotions that enable humans to 'connect' with the emotions of other HSs – are lacking in his case.[14] Nevertheless, these 'intellectually emotional' HSs find it easy to discuss somebody else's feelings with non-autistic HSs. If the other person can accurately describe those emotions in words, they become thoughts and ideas. An 'emotionally detached but intellectually present' autistic individual can give valuable advice, thus helping the other person to sort out his or her emotional baggage. Another bonus of this subgroup is their ability to feel joy due to their intellectual achievements. It's interesting that an 'intellectually emotional' person can become very 'emotionally emotional' under the effect of arts, literature, or films.

Emotional overload

Some autistic humans are very sensitive to emotional triggers. They may be easily overwhelmed with 'emotional tide-waves', resulting in overload. Another factor to be considered is difficulty in processing emotions at the time they are happening, leading to the delayed interpretation of emotions. Donna Williams introduces a metaphor of 'an emotional dirty laundry' that has been stored up to the point of overflow. Just keeping up with things, like a computer working to full capacity, there is no time for emotions to register at the time they are triggered by the situation. The feelings just pile up in the laundry room to be sorted and ironed later. But keeping them unprocessed in the room brings overload when the door eventually bursts open.[15] The *delayed emotions* phenomenon contributes to the difficulty in understanding them because if emotions are not interpreted in the context they happen it is hard to link them to the physical experience.

Emotional hypersensitivity

Temple Grandin describes the contradictory feeling of autistic children wanting to be held and experience the nice social feeling but often finding it too overwhelming as a tidal wave of sensation drowning them. She reflects on her child-hood memories of wanting to be hugged but experiencing panic because the sensation became so strong and powerful that her reaction was to pull away. Being touched by another person was so intense it was intolerable.[4] That's why some autistic kids would get under the mattresses or cushions in order to get comforting feelings and be able to control the pressure when it becomes too intense, but they would pull away and isolate themselves from other humans as the experi-ence might be too 'emotionally painful'.

Even if emotions are positive, autistic tolerance of 'emo-tional expression' of others can be very low. Loud praise, applause and noisy encouragement can frighten autistic children enormously. I always wonder when teachers and therapists do just that to an emotionally sensitive child, what do they want to achieve? Do they want this child to withdraw and never make an effort again? There is positive reinforce-ment and positive reinforcement. For an autistic child it should be given in the dose that particular child can cope with.

Another problem related to emotional hypersensitivity is difficulty in *stopping feeling*. Like difficulty in stopping feeling sensation long after the stimulus itself disappeared (for example, Alex's 'sticky' nails), some autistic humans may *feel* emotion long after the trigger disappears – I'd call it 'sticky emotions'. For example, Temple Grandin can't watch any violent movies with rape or torture scenes because these emotional pictures stay in her conscious mind for a very long time. It may be explained by her visual thinking. Even forcing herself to think about something else does not prevent bad images from popping up in her mind. To get rid of the pop-up images she has to click consciously on another screen.[4] It is one thing to think about 'torture' as a concept, and quite another, while thinking, to actually *see* a very specific incident of torture. A 'language filter' protects verbal thinkers from emotional overload. If this filter is absent, the impact of emotional involvement is much greater.

Emotional hyposensitivity

Here belongs the condition that is not specific to autism but some autistic humans may have it as well. This is alexithymia.

> *Alexithymia*: when humans are unable to put their feelings into words or to express their emotions in any other ways, though they are able to feel them.

The psychiatrist, Peter Sifneos, who coined this term, described these humans as giving the impression of being different, alien beings, having come from entirely different worlds, living in a society which is dominated by feelings.[16] Goleman clarifies that it is not that alexithymics never feel, but rather they are unable to describe their feelings. As one of the patients who cried while watching a movie put it: they feel awful but can't say exactly which kind of awful it is they feel.[16] The cause of alexithymia is not yet known.

~ ~ ~

The most common emotions (because they are most 'visible') in autism seem to be feelings of 'not belonging', fear, stress, anxiety, depression and anger. The fear of uncertainty is quite common. What will happen now? It's important to know and be prepared. Many autistic humans display high levels of anxiety. The causes of this unpleasant emotion are manifold – low self-esteem, fear of being misunderstood, rejection, fear of failure, confrontation with the environment that is unpredictable and confusing. Some have severe panic attacks. Miss Ponytail told Mother that since her teens she has become easily depressed because she feels alienated, rejected and lacking social life.

What about positive emotions? Do they feel happy? And an even more important question: Can they love their nearest and dearest? I've heard many parents of non-verbal autistic kids asking the same question again and again. Does my child love me? Their 'love me, love me not?' quest is heartbreaking and… meaningless. If they expect the autistic child to show love conventionally they will be very disappointed. Autistic humans express this feeling differently, but they are capable of loving unconditionally, deeply and truly.

Though both non-autistic and autistic HSs experience exactly the same basic emotions there are some differences as well. Non-autistic emotions often seem to be persistent and develop into a continuous emotional attitude. For example, anger turns into hatred that can last many years, if not a lifetime. For many autistic humans these emotions are situational: as soon as their anger diminishes, the negative emotion disappears without trace. They may often feel different emotions to non-autistic humans during the same event.[17] For instance, when non-autistic HSs enjoy certain activities, autistics may feel confused or frightened and vice versa. Alex may laugh at certain sounds or may amuse himself by repeating an action. What autistic HSs feel is invisible to outsiders. It may be like a private joke that the child keeps hearing in his or her head, and it makes the child giggle. Autistic children can relive instances vividly, be they positive or negative, using stored sensory bits in the brain.[17]

Autistic emotions are often deep and intense. (This is not reflected in the common assumption that 'autistic people lack emotions'.) Autistic people do feel happy, or sad, or angry. For instance, when Temple Grandin was a child and other kids teased her, she felt very upset.[18] Temple Grandin derives great emotional satisfaction from her career of designing livestock equipment. She is happy when a client is pleased with the facility she designed. When one of her projects failed or a client criticised her unfairly Temple became depressed and upset. Her emotional satisfaction from doing something that is of value to society is very real, very powerful. Why don't humans listen? Nobody can feel what somebody else is feeling, but they can empathise.

> *Empathy*: the ability to identify oneself mentally with somebody else, thus understanding what this person feels.

> *Sympathy*: the state of being simultaneously affected with a feeling to that of another person – the ability to share the emotion.

I've read many books about autism and nine out of ten contain erroneous information about empathy in autism. Many authors claim that autistic humans lack empathy and are unable to understand others' perspectives. Knowing perceptual and cognitive differences, language and communication problems in autism, isn't it more fair to claim that autistic HSs do not share others' experiences and that is why they have difficulty in understanding them? Besides, autistic humans may have difficulties expressing and receiving communicative signals that further complicate the matter. But lack of empathy? I wouldn't meow so. Some high-functioning autistic HSs make a lot of effort to understand the perspectives of non-autistic humans. They do not make any assumptions and check their perceptions all the time. (Yes, sometimes it is irritating, when Alex asks his Mother 'Are you angry? Please don't get cross.' When he misreads Mother's facial expression he wants to be sure that she feels fine.)

In contrast, many non-autistic HSs assume that they understand the perspective of somebody with autism without taking any trouble to find out this person's real inspirations and motivations. There is a residential unit for autistic adults in our area. When I took up the challenge of writing this book and conducting my research in autism I made it a habit to pop into the residential home to check what was going on there. On the first day of my 'inspection' one particular member of staff was on duty. (I call him 'Arrogant-Know-All'.) He was talking to a new member of staff about the service-users.

'Nick in room 3 never goes out. He doesn't like any outside activities. We let him stay in his room...'

The new girl (whom I call 'Don't-Know-Much-But-Want-to-Learn') interrupted him, 'How do you know?'

Arrogant-Know-All jumped to his feet: the lack of respect for his 'knowledge and expertise' from someone who was new to the service made him furious.

'If you want to work here, you'd better learn to listen to your superiors. I've been working here for more than ten years. I know what my clients think and what they want!'

It was too depressing for me to listen to this 'educational' conversation. I turned to the path leading home and literally bumped into MtheD who had nothing else to do and was mingling around, looking for trouble. Her greeting wasn't very friendly.

'Hey, you, so-called researcher. Trespassing?'

'Researching. What are you doing here? Trespassing?'

I should have known better than to contradict her, or even worse, to joke about *her* trespassing (but we were at the same spot: if one was trespassing, so was the other – Right? Wrong!). Anyone without personality problems would agree with my line of thinking, but MtheD was different.

'How dare you! You have slandered my character! You said that I am a burglar!'

'But I didn't! You misunderstood me...'

'You did! You did! I understood you perfectly well. You thought that I was here to burgle this house. You said that I was a criminal. Apologise!'

'Listen, MtheD. Please calm down. You asked me if I was trespassing and I...'

'You think you can walk wherever you want and I have to be locked up in a cage.'

'You got it wrong. I...'

'Oh, yes, I got it right. You think if I am not well educated, I have no right to criticise you. It's democracy here, if you don't know. I'll show you your place. I'll tell every creature in the neighbourhood that you are a disrespectful, shameful, deceitful member of the feline community, and that you attacked me!'

She fled to start her campaign to protect the community from so-called felines who... I found out the details the next day – her 'smelly messages' were all over the place – fences, trees, window sills, doors... Wrong assumptions can lead to many unpleasant (and unfair) experiences.

In contrast to non-autistic humans with personality disorders, many autistic HSs have a very strong sense of social justice and a lot of compassion for others. Miss Ponytail has ended up in difficult situations many times, just because she always tries to defend those who are mistreated or disadvantaged. Temple Grandin can provide an objective evaluation of another scientist's work even if she hates him as a person.[18] (How many non-autistic HSs can do that?) Some high-functioning autistic humans may lack 'affective empathy' because they have difficulty reading the signals, but compensate for it with 'cognitive/intellectual empathy', trying (and in many cases succeeding) to understand what it is like to experience the same as someone else experiences, or, how some humans will phrase it, to wear someone else's shoes. (Absolutely incomprehensible for me. Why do you need shoes, I wonder?)

CHAPTER **10**

Challenging Behaviours: Who Challenges Whom?

You won't find a book about autism that doesn't mention 'challenging behaviours'. In older books they go under the terms 'problem behaviours', 'difficult behaviours', or 'inappropriate behaviours' but mean exactly the same thing. Some non-autistic humans include in this category any behaviour that is different from the norm. I think this isn't fair, because some behaviours are absolutely *normal* autistic behaviours if you take into account their way of processing information and acting on it. The fact that some behaviours may be difficult (challenging) not only for the non-autistic population but also for autistic humans is another matter altogether. That is why I have come up with my own classification and working definitions of challenging behaviours, and designed my research to find the answers to very important questions:

- What behaviours are 'challenging'?

- Why are they challenging?

- Whom do they challenge?

- What is to be done to 'unchallenge' challenging behaviours?

I classify all the difficult behaviours into three large groups:

- challenging behaviours (proper)
- unchallenging behaviours
- challenging unchallenging behaviours

Challenging behaviours

Challenging behaviours: behaviours which interfere either with the wellbeing of the person who displays these behaviours, or other humans' wellbeing, or both.

These behaviours challenge:

- the person who displays them: for instance, pica (eating inedible substances such as earth, stones or grass, etc.) can bring a lot of health problems to the person, or self-injury

- other humans who are in contact with the person: for example, aggression towards them, switching lights on and off, making noises or running around in the classroom when other students are working, and just creating havoc in public places

- both the person and others. Some behaviours that *seem* to challenge only 'the others' are in fact challenging for the person him/herself. They often don't want to do them but cannot help it, for example, during panic attacks they may become aggressive towards others, not because they want to hurt the person, but because they cannot control their outburst.

Let us take one example of this type of behaviour: self-abuse or self-injury. It is frightening yet it has its reasons and may be caused by several things.[1] For example, autistic humans with severe sensory problems can sometimes engage in self-injurious behaviour. Their sensory sensations may be so disordered that they may not realise that they are hurting themselves.[2] Even if they do feel pain from head-banging, for example, at least they know they are in control, while the confusion and pain inflicted by the environment is uncontrollable. Self-abuse may be a result of fear and anger, when the child is punished for his or her involuntary response to the situation, but doesn't understand why.[1] Puberty often makes the problems worse. Some teenagers can develop unpredictable screaming fits and tantrums. The hormones further inflame an overaroused nervous system.[2]

These behaviours should be addressed for the sake of the person him/herself and other HSs (and nHSs) involved. The way to treat them depends on each individual's underlying causes. In some cases there may be 'medical reasons' (imbalance of immune system, inflammatory guts, allergies, etc.) that can be addressed, for instance with diets or special supplements. Some behaviours, however, must be removed from the list of difficult behaviours if they cannot be classified under the definition above. I'd call them 'unchallenging behaviours'.

Unchallenging behaviours

> *Unchallenging behaviours:* behaviours that do not interfere with other humans' wellbeing and do not cause any health, physical or psychological problems to the autistic person, and do not interfere with his/her quality of life. They may look bizarre or weird but are actually harmless to others and pleasurable to the person.

Examples of these are rocking, flapping, lining up objects, touching or tapping objects, producing sounds, gazing at the hands and other similar behaviours that makes the person feel better or are just pleasurable activities. Jasmine O'Neill writes a lot about the reasons and functions of 'stimmies', which are *not* a behavioural problem and shouldn't be disciplined.[1]

> *Stims*: self-stimulatory stereotyped behaviours, for example, flapping hands, rocking the body, rubbing skin, blinking, producing rhythmical noises, etc.

For example, a child runs past a stationary object, peeking at it as he runs by. He may be intrigued by the way its appearance is changed by his own movements. He is exploring his environment, learning about spatial relations and enjoying physical sensations. For many autistic children self-stimulation can be a way to burn away their nervous energy and calm themselves. Trying to make them give up their stims for another way of comfort that is more acceptable can be painful and seen as a threat.[1] Stims do *look* strange for non-autistic HSs, but when I think about it, non-autistic HSs have strange behaviours themselves and do nothing about them. For example, what is the point of asking someone how he or she is feeling if they are not interested in his or her medical history? Isn't it bizarre? On the other paw, what is wrong with rocking your body and humming while in your own bedroom?

The same is true about animals' 'difficult behaviours', which are actually normal behaviours interpreted as a problem in an 'abnormal' context. I've mentioned this many times already (maybe because it hurts so much to be misunderstood by the humans who are very special to me). It's normal for a cat to kill rodents and other small animals and bring them to the place which is my home. OK, I do understand Mother's sensitivities to the sight of dead bodies and

I've got used to her acrobatic exercises when she sees one, but to call me names (the most common one being 'Murderess!') just because I'm a normal cat, is over the top. Yes, it does hurt!

Stims belong to the group of behaviours caused by differences in sensory functioning. To describe these behaviours I'll borrow the word 'sensorisms' from Olga Bogdashina[3] who, in turn, borrowed it from Carl Delacato's work,[4] removing one letter to make it easier to pronounce: from 'sensoryisms' to 'sensorisms'.

> *Sensorisms*: behaviours caused by the way senses receive and interpret information. Differences in sensory perception bring different reactions (sensorisms) to the same stimuli. For example, avoiding eye contact (peripheral perception), shutting the eyes while listening to something (monoprocessing), stims.

Sensorisms may serve several purposes, and one and the same behaviour may have different underlying causes. From my research and very close observation of quite a few autistic humans in my neighbourhood, I would identify several functions of sensorisms (the list is far from complete):

- Defensive (to reduce the pain or discomfort caused by hypersensitivities, fragmentation, overload, and other sensory perceptual difficulties). In this case, stims help eliminate a sensory overload that interferes with functioning.

- Self-stimulatory (for example, to improve the input in the case of hyposensitivity).

- Compensatory (to interpret the environment in the case of unreliable sensory information). Stims can be reactions to all the bombardment and confusion.

- To shut the world out. When autistic humans become overloaded, spinning and rocking make them calm. However, these behaviours may become addictive. The more they do it, the more they want to do it.[5]

- Out of frustration. Sometimes head-banging, tantrums and outbursts are the only means available to them to let others know that enough is enough.[6]

Should humans aim to 'fix up' all these behaviours, i.e. to get rid of all the sensorisms? I don't think so. No matter how irritating and meaningless these behaviours seem to non-autistic HSs, it is unwise to stop them without learning the function they serve and introducing experiences with the same function.

We animals also have stims. Some of them, like purring or kneading, for example, increase our calm and feel good. Others, like pacing the cage in captivity, are caused by boredom and lack of stimulation. These self-stimulatory activities mean that the animal is unhappy. Humans must address this issue as soon as possible. The simplest solution will be to set the animals free in their natural habitat. If this is impossible, they should be provided not only with food but also with social life and a lot of activities they can choose from. But back to autism.

Stereotypies caused by sensory processing problems must be addressed, but not on the surface: it's not enough to make the child stop flapping his or her hands, for example. It's important to interpret these behaviours. And here we have a problem. One of the difficulties in interpreting the autistic person's behaviour caused by sensory processing differences is the carer's non-autistic sensory function. It's important to imagine (if not fully comprehend) how the person perceives the world and help the person develop strategies to cope with these (often painful) sensitivities. The carers and professionals working with autistic humans have to train themselves to perceive and understand the world from the person's perspective (the way I've done it with Alex). Only then will they join those they live or work with 'on his/her territory', in his/her perceptual world and will not have to live in two parallel ones.

Challenging unchallenging behaviours

Challenging unchallenging behaviours: behaviours which are involuntary, unintentional, not under the person's control. They either bring frustration and the feeling of helplessness or make the person give up any attempt to express him/herself.

There are at least two subtypes of the 'challenging unchallenging' behaviours in autism. Sometimes autistic humans cannot control their behaviours, either challenging or unchallenging ones. They don't want to do them but cannot help it because these behaviours are involuntary, triggered by certain environmental or internal factors. The situation becomes worse when other humans 'misread' these involuntary responses, and either explain them as 'pleasurable activities' that should be encouraged (bringing more frustration to the individual) or blame the person for being 'difficult' on purpose (which makes the person feel guilt and self-hatred for the inability to control him/herself). Donna Williams describes the frustration they feel when other humans reprimand them and blame them for something not under their control. Other humans' misunderstanding (words and actions) just trigger more unintentional (and challenging) behaviours like, for example, aggression or self-injury.[7]

Sometimes 'unchallenging' behaviours which seem to be harmless or even beneficial and pleasurable for the person may turn into challenging and undesirable (for the person) activities. *Any* unchallenging behaviour that starts as a purposeful self-stimulation but turns into an all-absorbing activity, hindering the development of the person, belongs to this group. Some autistic humans may become addicted to certain stims, and the more they do it, the more they want to do it. In this case, the explanation that the person has the right to do what he or she wants to do ('leave them alone!') is a politically correct but practically wrong one. There are autistic humans who do *not* appreciate involuntary responses happening to them. These stims may be counterproductive; they are not the same as intended self-expression that comes from choice; they have nothing to do with personality or identity and the 'right to be autistic'.[7] Because of this, is it wise to encourage these 'challenging unchallenging' behaviours, instead of helping the individual find ways to express him/herself?

There are dozens of (both challenging and 'unchallenging', and 'challenging unchallenging') behaviours that are quite common in autism. Some humans call them 'autistic behaviours'. I don't think this is meaningful because, first, some 'autistic behaviours' may be displayed by non-autistic humans as well (like pacing or tapping when they are bored or anxious); second, one and the same behaviour can originate from several different causes, and it's unhelpful to throw them all into one pile without identifying the function and the cause of each behaviour. This topic is so complicated that I decided to write a research paper for our peer-reviewed message board and publish it on the lamp post around the corner from my house. Polly was the first to review it and was very much impressed with my academic abilities. Here is my article translated into English humanese.

ABC vs. understanding

There is a very popular ABC (Antecedent–Behaviour–Consequence) approach when the carer is supposed to find the trigger (Antecedent), define the Behaviour and provide the Consequence for this (often called inappropriate) behaviour – ignore/time out/etc. In autism this approach does not always work. Sometimes the antecedent cannot be easily identified, because it can be either 'present but invisible', or 'possible future', or 'past' antecedent. Let me explain.

Present but invisible antecedent

Sometimes the carers cannot see/hear/feel certain stimuli as their senses are too 'normal'. For example, the child may be disturbed by the sound of the microwave oven two rooms away. As the carer cannot hear it, any 'challenging behaviour' displayed by the child would be interpreted as 'out of the blue'.

Possible future antecedent

Not only certain stimuli but also any sudden unpredictable stimuli can be painful. The fear of a stimulus that 'hurts' is often the cause of challenging behaviours. The antecedents cannot be easily identified because they are 'possible future antecedents'. Some autistic children may try to break things (for example, telephone or alarm clock) that can produce unpredictable painful sound. They do it as a protective reaction. For instance, when younger, Alex could not tolerate babies crying. Even when a baby was asleep he would try to attack (hit or kick) it. I do sympathise with the poor babies and their mothers who (understandably) were not very happy with his behaviour. (Fortunately for the unsuspecting parties, Alex's mother managed to prevent the disastrous outcome.

Well, in most cases, anyway.) The trigger (antecedent) was 'in the future'. It was easier for Alex to tolerate the cry, when he was prepared for it and could see the source of it. This explains his 'challenging' behaviour – to initiate and be in control of the painful sounds, make them predictable, instead of jumping out of his skin when the baby starts crying and he does not expect it.

Past antecedent

Sometimes any stimuli (not only sensory but also emotional ones) may bring the memories of pain, or anger, or panic (happened in the past). As any memory brought to the surface (i.e. to consciousness) becomes very much 'present', the person may react the way he or she reacted in the past, when the bad experience happened. What can provoke anger, fear, anxiety, panic attack? Anything! From smell to emotionally coloured intonations. For instance, some smells may bring pleasurable memories, and other odours remind one of unhappy ones. Or take another trigger – an emotional aspect of a word. Some words have emotional colouring, others can be negatively charged. In autism, the conventional interpretation doesn't matter. If something unpleasant happened when the child heard the word 'sorry', for example, he would connect this word with the experience. Any time the child hears 'Sorry!' he may react with rage – the experience repeats itself.

The 'last straw' antecedent

Sometimes there are no definite triggers whatsoever. The cause of the challenging behaviour may be *overload*, i.e. if the person has been struggling already, anything can be the last straw. Their sensory perceptual inconsistencies and differences can make dealing with the environment very difficult. They may become overloaded in situations that would not bother other humans. This may result in several scenarios:

- Sensory agnosia (or difficulty interpreting a sense) is a sort of 'literal perception', when interpretation of any sense can be lost. Though they can see/hear, etc. adequately, they may often have limited comprehension of what is being seen/heard, etc. It is a very frightening experience.[3]

- If they continue to try to process all the information coming in, despite their inability to keep up with it, it may result in hypersensitivity and/or fragmentation that eventually bring anxiety, confusion, frustration and stress, that in turn lead to tantrums and difficult behaviours.

The signs of coming overload are very individual. For example, when Alex is 'nearly there' his lips become so thin that they look like a line, his movements get twitchy, and his eyes are just 'empty'. Mother easily recognises these signs (she's learned them the hard way), but there are two problems: first, the time between the first signs and Alex's outburst is less than a minute (she cannot do much in crowded places – one minute is not enough to find a quiet spot and take him there); second, she is not always with him, and other carers may not notice the signs before it is too late. To address these shortcomings she teaches Alex to recognise the internal signs and either ask for help (when he is still in control), or use different strategies (like relaxation techniques or removing himself from the situation) to prevent the problem. Alex's friend David is different. When he experiences overload and his rage becomes uncontrollable, he would attack first the furniture and then… himself. To protect him from self-injury, David wears a helmet, as he tends to bang his head against the furniture or the walls (whichever is nearer).

~ ~ ~

The good news is that those with challenging behaviours have great potential for development. They are motivated to 'belong' and understand the world around them. It seems a terrible thing to state this, but it's true in many cases that it's much easier to withdraw from the environment and live in their own world than to try to cope with the real one. It is more difficult to reach someone who has given up, who has retreated into what Donna Williams calls the sanctuary of autism, the world inside themselves.[7] There is neither motivation nor desire to let the others in or join them in their world. Strangely enough, some teachers like to 'work' with these withdrawn, passive children who are happy to sit in the corner of the classroom from morning till afternoon when it's time to go home. The (uninformed) professionals think it's easy to help these children, as there are 'no challenging behaviours'. They are right about the absence of 'problem behaviours'. But the side effect is that there is no motivation to participate in the activities either. It's not only about children, but also about adults with autism. For example, the staff in the residential service for autistic adults (which I inspect on a weekly basis) are very proud of their approach to provide choices for their clients. The problem is that some of the clients have had very little experiences outside their rooms. What can they choose from? 'Stay all day in my room' or 'stay all day in my room'? Of course, they 'choose' the only option they have had experience with because they don't know anything else. Whenever there is an inspection (not by me, but by humans) of this service, the staff proudly reply to any question: 'So-and-so has chosen to stay in his room today. We respect his choice.' On the other paw, those who are motivated to learn, to get new experiences are (illogically) considered 'difficult'. They are difficult because they want to be with other HSs, not isolate themselves in their own world. And the reward they often get? Either medication turning them into zombies or isolation in hospitals, or both. Fortunately, some HSs are sapient enough to understand this. Usually, these are parents or those professionals who know their clients really well. They can interpret 'challenging behaviours' correctly – not as personal attacks, but the inability to cope with the world around them.

Take Alex, for example. His parents do their best to give him as many experiences as possible (in small doses). Being an eager participant in all the family activities, Alex tries to do his best to cope in difficult circumstances. Sometimes it goes wrong and they make mistakes. For instance, after he enjoyed a very long film (Harry Potter 1) in the cinema, his family decided to build on this success and took him to the movies again. But the choice they made was very unfortunate, and they regretted it 40 minutes into the film. There were too many bright lights and loud sounds (car crashes, shooting and shouting). In the middle of the film there were two battles to win – one on the screen between good guys and villains, and the other in the auditorium – between Alex, who couldn't cope with too much stimulation but wanted to stay with his family, and his mother who tried to persuade him to go out. The public seemed to be more interested in the outcomes of the second battle than the first one, and too much attention didn't help. Alex was kicking the seat in front of him and shouting 'Stop it! Stop it!' To make a long story short, the whole family eventually managed to escort Alex outside, just when the main villain pointed the gun at the good guy. I do hope there was a happy ending in the film, though I cannot be certain – the family decided not to watch this film ever again – out of principle.

Our Alex (and others like him) challenges himself: he wants to be a part of his family, a part of his community, a part of mankind. Till he was seven and had no verbal language or didn't know any conventional way to communicate, Alex was either an aloof child living in his own world or, when he dared to come out but couldn't cope with the environment, he exhibited challenging behaviours – behaviours challenging his family, and the boy himself. So after each unsuccessful attempt to 'get out', he retreated back into his sanctuary where he could relax and forget about everything and everybody. From what I can see now, Alex has made his choice and it is a well-informed one because he's got the experiences of both worlds. He wants to be with others, while being himself, processing information and responding to the world in his own unique way. He ignores both the 'thought police' ('one bad word about autism and you are out!') and some pessimistic HSs ('autism is a curse'). Those around him try to help him adjust to the mainstream environment while making necessary adjustments to meet his needs. Efforts from both sides are vital. To recognise strengths (to be developed) and weaknesses (to be treated) is a start. What is more important is to be realistic and respectful of others. This is the way forward. It will be difficult but with understanding and learning from each other, Alex and those who love him are determined to do the best they can. Even if he won't be able to live independently and will always need some support, his life will be meaningful and happy. The family (led by me, of course) and our friends will make sure it will become possible.

And there is the last (but not the least) challenge I want to write about. This time I, as a representative of the United Kingdom of non-Human Animals, am challenging Human Animals. Often humans' behaviour towards animals is inappropriate, difficult, challenging and wrong. These behaviours include (but are not limited to): cruelty; killing animals just for fun; using animals for experiments; keeping animals in captivity (sometimes in terrible conditions); making them perform for the crowds and so on. I haven't included one challenging behaviour of humans that some animals would – eating meat. Many people eat meat. They breed cattle and chicken (not to mention turkey for Christmas), for example, for food. I cannot comment on this issue, because I am not a vegetarian, either. I think that nature and evolution take care of diets of different species. Some have developed into plant-eating creatures, others into meat-eaters, and still others' menu consists of both meat and vegetables. All animals (both humans and non-humans) must eat to survive. Humans can make a choice about what to eat and become vegetarians on moral, religious or cultural ground (though some humans have to eat meat because of metabolic or other health problems). Animals, however, lack such a privilege: they eat what their genetic blueprints prescribe them to eat. And yes, predators kill smaller and weaker animals for food. I wouldn't criticise them and, unlike Mother, I wouldn't call them names. But humans are often illogical, aren't they? Sometimes they kill each other as well, and not for survival but for other, not very honourable, reasons. I've come to the conclusion that some Homo sapiens are not very 'sapient', not because they are not intelligent enough, but because they use their intelligence to harm others. One non-sapient human can destroy a country, two (non-sapient ones) can destroy the world. Animals cannot compete with it.

What is absolutely unacceptable is the cruelty some HSs display towards nHSs: killing for fun, breeding animals in terrible conditions for their fur or meat, making them suffer, and using them for experiments. Why do some humans think it's OK to *use* animals for their own purpose? Let us apply the

ABC approach. Where are the Antecedents of these cruel Behaviours, I wonder? What have we done to deserve this treatment? And the Consequences may be disastrous. (The world without animals would be a sad place to live in.) I'm not going to write about this – it is too upsetting, but I wouldn't side up with some humans who claim to defend animal rights, using very cruel methods, either. You cannot defeat cruelty with cruelty. There must be other ways to achieve the same goal. I wish all HSs understand that the better they treat animals, the more human they become.

There is another human behaviour directed at animals (usually domesticated ones) that theoretically is an 'un-challenging challenging' behaviour but in practice it turns into 'challenging unchallenging' manipulation. I am referring to treating us pets as toys or babies: for example, dressing dogs or cats in ridiculous outfits, hats, boots and ribbons; taking them to pets' hairdressers for ludicrous treatments; parading them in front of other humans, and the like. The purpose of it (Antecedent) is twofold: pets look cute and their owners feel better about themselves. The outcome (Consequence) is that pets become toys. There are better ways to be happy about themselves and their furry friends. For example, animals can (literally) treat humans in pet therapy (both parties win!). Animals are known as therapists for treating depression in humans, being good company for an autistic individual, or even trained to warn the humans about coming seizures. The psychological support potential of animals is difficult to overestimate. In short, both nHSs and HSs can 'live happily ever after'.

~ ~ ~

In the beginning of my journal I promised to disclose my first (and very powerful) reason for becoming a writer. So here it is.

My first reason for writing this book is the one that may actually prevent it from publication. To be quite honest, I don't care whether it will be published or not. The only thing I really want is to receive the proofs – yes, these piles of paper that publishers send to the author for proof-reading and indexing. What can be better than curling up on A4 sheets on the table, feeling the warmth and softness of the paper? The paper that does not make you sink in a hole but holds your body with strength and tenderness at the same time. You wouldn't understand it if you've never experienced it.

Dasha aka Furry Paperweight

Dreaming of a happy ending

Dasha's Glossary

Alexithymia is the condition where humans are unable to put their feelings into words or to express their emotions in any other ways, though they are able to feel them.

Anthropomorphism is the attribution of human behaviour or personality to non-human animals.

> **Felinism** is the attribution of cat behaviour or personality to non-feline (usually human) animals. You wish!

> **Caninism** is the attribution of dog behaviour or personality to non-canine (usually human) animals.

Bast and Sekhmet are two Egyptian 'feline Goddesses'. Bast is the Goddess of Lower Egypt and protector of cats, women and children. Typically she is depicted as a young woman with the head of a cat. Another popular depiction of Bast is her earthly form, as a seated cat. (When in this form her name changes to Bastet.) Sekhmet is the Goddess of Upper Egypt, depicted as a woman with the head of a lioness.

Birdbrain is a derogative term used by HSs to mean 'a stupid person'. In fact, the inability to grasp the intelligence of birds makes HSs look mentally retarded themselves.

Challenging behaviours are behaviours which interfere either with the wellbeing of the person who displays these behaviours, or other humans' wellbeing, or both.

'**Challenging unchallenging' behaviours** are behaviours which are involuntary, unintentional, not under the person's control. They either bring frustration and the feeling of helplessness or make the person give up any attempt to express him/herself.

Cognition is a general term for mental processes by which sensory information is interpreted, stored and used.

Communication is transmission of information between individuals.

Co-morbid condition in plain English is a condition/disorder that co-occurs with any other condition. In an 'autism-is-beautiful' interpretation, co-morbid disorder is anything negative about autism.

Concept is an abstract idea or mental image of a group or class of objects formed by combining their aspects. For example, cats of different colours, breeds, sizes (like Dasha, Sally, MtheD, etc.) all go under the same heading 'a cat'.

Deictic words are words that 'cannot stay still'; they jump from one object or place to the other, depending where the person who uses them stands. For example, 'here–there': what is 'here' for you is 'there' for someone at the other side of the room; 'this–that': you are reading 'this' book but it suddenly becomes 'that' book for someone who is in the kitchen, for example.

Echolalia is the parrot-like repetition of another person's spoken words. There are usually two distinguishable types of echolalia: **immediate echolalia** (or repetition of words and phrases just heard), e.g. Mother: 'Do you want an ice-cream?' Child: 'You want an ice-cream'; and **delayed echolalia** (or repetition of words and phrases heard in the past), e.g. when having a meal the child announces, 'May the Force be with you!'

Emotions are interpretations of feelings when both somatic and affective feelings are experienced as a kind of sensory–perceptual input with cognitive explanation and conscious plan of action.

Empathy is the ability to identify oneself mentally with somebody else, thus understanding what this person feels.

Ethologist is a scientist who studies animal behaviour. The word ethology originated from Greek *ēthos* 'nature, disposition' and is not restricted to non-human animals but includes *all* species (humans included). In this sense the best human ethologists are cats who detect the patterns of each character very easily and use this knowledge to manipulate their humans.

Feelings are physical sensations. They can be **somatic** and **affective**.

    Somatic experiences are feelings of the body, for example, muscle tension, tiredness, headache, chest pain, goose bumps, etc.

    Affective experiences are feelings of the soul, for example, emptiness, panic, etc.

Homo sapiens (HS) is from the Latin 'Man Wise' or Wise Man, or human being.

Idioms are groups of words that do not mean what they really mean. You have to look behind the literal meaning and learn the hidden message of each expression. Non-autistic HSs use idioms in order to confuse autistic people.

'I-ness' (Synonyms: *self-consciousness, self-awareness*): awareness of being 'I' and experiencing being alive, doing things and perceiving what is happening to I.

Intelligence is the understanding of the world, the ability to think about it and act on it.

IQ tests are tests designed to measure intelligence.

Language is typically defined as a system of symbols and methods of combination of these symbols that serves as a means of communication and formulating and expressing thoughts.

Metaphor is a descriptive word that is applied to an object or an action, even if it has nothing to do with it! To understand metaphors you have to forget about the literal meanings of words and use your imagination. For example, 'cat-eyed' or 'cat eye' doesn't mean 'somebody with cat eyes', but rather 'somebody able to see in the dark'.

Narcissism is self-love, self-admiration, self-centredness. A small amount of narcissistic traits is healthy but too much narcissism turns into **pathological narcissism**, i.e. thinking 'I am the best', intolerance of others' views, overestimation of one's abilities, disregard for the needs and feelings of others.

Neologism is a new word or expression created to name something that has not yet the definition in one's vocabulary. For example, Alex created the word 'paintlipster' to mean 'lipstick'.

Percept is a mental image resulting from perceiving. For example, a visual image of me (visual percept), or the feeling of my fur on the hand (a tactile image), or the sound of my purring (auditory image) when the word 'cat' is heard.

Pet shop is a place where humans come to be adopted by the animals who are brave enough to take responsibility for looking after them. Oh, and you can buy food and all the living necessities there too. Humans don't eat healthy food and their homes lack vital equipment, such as, for example, scratching posts or toys to keep mind and body fit. In a way, animals bring civilisation into the primitive living conditions of their pets. So those fortunate humans who have been adopted suddenly find their lives improving tremendously.

Sensorisms are behaviours caused by the way senses receive and interpret information. Differences in sensory perception bring different reactions (sensorisms) to the same stimuli. For example, avoiding eye contact (peripheral perception), shutting the eyes while listening to something (monoprocessing), **stims**.

Stims are self-stimulatory stereotyped behaviours, for example, flapping hands, rocking the body, rubbing skin, blinking, producing rhythmical noises, etc.

Sympathy is the state of being simultaneously affected with a feeling to that of another person; the ability to share the emotion.

Synaesthesia is the ability to perceive stimulation of one sense via a different sensory modality. For example, I see 'red' when I hear dogs barking.

Synonyms are two or more (very different) words with the same meaning, e.g. 'cat', 'puss' and 'feline' mean 'Dasha' (i.e. me). The meaning is the same but sometimes synonyms may differ in neutrality/formality and emotional colouring. For instance, when you approach me as a researcher it's better to call me 'feline'; if you don't want to be too formal, you may call me a 'cat'. My family and my friends may call me Dasha. (Don't call me 'puss' – I don't like it!)

Thinking is using thoughts.

Trilogue is a conversation between two persons, i.e. a dialogue, ignoring the presence of a third party because: (a) it's a young child who is not supposed to understand what adults are talking about; (b) it's a disabled person who is not supposed to understand what 'normal' people are talking about; (c) it's an animal who is not supposed to understand what humans are talking about. Contrary to this wrong assumption, the third party present – whether (a), (b), or (c) – actually contributes (mentally) to the dialogue, thus creating a trilogue.

Umwelt means the specific world of any given animal (humans included).

'Unchallenging' behaviours are behaviours that do not interfere with other humans' wellbeing and do not cause any health, physical or psychological problems to the autistic person, and do not interfere with his/her quality of life. They may look bizarre or weird but actually are harmless to the others and pleasurable to the person.

Notes and References

Chapter 2: Disclaimer

1. Six years of cat age correspond to 40 years human age (Taylor, D. (2004) *Think Cat: An Owner's Guide to Feline Psychology*. London: Cassell Illustrated.)

Chapter 3: What is Autism? That's the Question

1. Wing, L. (1996) *The Autistic Spectrum: A Guide for Parents and Professionals*. London: Constable.

2. Box 3.1: The Theory of Feline Mind Test:

   1. b: A cat rubs against the legs with its head, flank and tail, marking the human with her own scent and picking up some of the 'human smell messages', mixing her scent with the human's.
   2. a: It is important for a cat to establish and mark her territory, which, of course, goes further than the washing machine.
   3. b: After rubbing up against different objects at home, the cat would groom herself to read the information she has picked up and get the reassurance that everything is fine. Besides, rubbing involves writing messages for other cats to let them know that the territory is occupied.

3. Ghaziuddin, M. (2005) *Mental Health Aspects of Autism and Asperger Syndrome*. London: Jessica Kingsley Publishers.

Chapter 4: Animals and Humans, Cats and Dogs... What are You Trying to Meow?

1. *Amicus Plato sed magis amica veritas.* Plato is a friend but truth is yet a greater friend.

2. Grandin, T. and Johnson, C. (2005) *Animals in Translation: Using the Mysteries of Autism to Decode Animal Behavior.* London: Bloomsbury.

3. Zulueta, F. cited in Shaikh, T. (16 February 2006) 'Elephants never forget... and cannot forgive', *Times On-Line.* Available at www.timesonline.co.uk/tol/news/world/article731367.ece, accessed on 19 November 2007.

4. Prince-Hughes, D. (2004) *Songs of the Gorilla Nation: My Journey through Autism.* London: Souvenir Press.

5. Greenberg, J. (2006) *Monkey Portraits.* New York: Bulfinch Press.

6. Goodall, J. (2001) 'Foreword.' In S. M. Wise, *Rattling the Cage.* New York: Perseus Books.

7. Menzel, E. W. (1970) 'Cognitive Mapping in Chimpanzees.' In S. H. Hulse, H. Fowler and W. F. Honig (eds) *Cognitive Processes in Animal Behavior.* Hillsdale, NJ: Erlbaum.

8. Fitch, W. T. and Hauser, M. D. (2004) 'Computational constraints on syntactic processing in a nonhuman primate.' *Science 303,* 377–80.

9. Wise, S. M. (2001) *Rattling the Cage.* New York: Perseus Books.

10. Patterson, F. and Linden, E. (1988) *The Education of Koko.* New York: Henry Holt.

11. Patterson, F. (1986) 'The Mind of the Gorilla: Conversation and Conservation.' In K. Benirschke (ed) *Primates: The Road to Self-sustaining Population.* New York: Springer-Verlag.

12. Box 4.1: The nHS IQ Test

    1. Bees can use dance to communicate to their hive members the direction to the food source in relation to the position of the sun.
    2. Birds can see four different basic colours (ultraviolet, blue, green and red); people see three (blue, green and red).
    3. Some animals have very good night vision.
    4. Elephants use seismic means to communicate with other elephants as far away as 20 miles (O'Connell-Rodwell, C.

cited in Grandin, T. and Johnson, C. (2005) *Animals in Translation: Using the Mysteries of Autism to Decode Animal Behavior.* London: Bloomsbury, p.60).

5.   The Arctic tern can, *Ibid,* p.285).

6.   Grey squirrel can (*Ibid,* p.287).

7.   Bouvier des Flandres dogs can (*Ibid,* p.288).

13. Janik, V. M., Sayigh, L. S. and Wells, R. S. (2006) 'Signature Whistle Shape Conveys Identity Information to Bottlenose Dolphins.' *Proceedings of the National Academy of Sciences, USA 103:* 8293–97.

14. Pepperburg, I. M. (2000) *The Alex Studies: Cognitive and Communicative Abilities of Grey Parrots.* Cambridge, MA: Harvard University Press.

15. Dobson, R. (2006) 'Clever boy! Sheep recognise faces. They self-medicate. They're clever, dammit...' *Independent Online Edition,* 21 May 2006. Available at http://findarticles.com/p/articles/mi_qn4159/is_20060521/ai _n16415449, accessed on 19 November 2007.

16. Anderson, J. R. (1984) 'The development of self-recognition: A review.' *Developmental Psychology 17,* 1, 35–49.

17. Franks, N. (2006) 'Teaching in tandem-running ants.' *Nature 153,* 12 January 2006. Available at www.nature.com/nature/journal/v439/n7073/abs/439153a.ht ml, accessed on 19 November 2007.

18. Schwartz, G. E. and Russek, Linda G. S. (1999) *The Living Energy Universe.* Charlottesville, VA: Hampton Roads Publishing Co.

19. MacLean, P. D. (1990) *The Triune Brain in Evolution: Role in Paleocerebral Functions.* New York: Kluwer Academic Publishers.

20. Grandin, T. and Johnson, C. (2005) *Animals in Translation: Using the Mysteries of Autism to Decode Animal Behavior.* London: Bloomsbury, p.57.

21. Gould, J. L. and Gould, C. G. (1994) *The Animal Mind.* New York: Scientific American Library.

22. Page, G. (1999) *The Singing Gorilla: Understanding Animal Intelligence.* London: Headline Book Publishing.

23. Differences have been described in the cerebral cortex, the limbic system (the amygdala and hippocampus), the cerebellum and the

brainstem. The problem is that each of the differences has been seen in some but not all humans with autism.

24. The number of minicolumns is defined during the first 40 days of fetal gestation. The small and numerous minicolumns in the brains of autistic individuals favour information processing through intraregional pathways (this accounts for the abilities of many autistic people to excel at mathematical calculation and visual processing) while cognitive functions that require long interregional connections (for example, verbal language, face recognition, joint attention) would prove metabolically inefficient (Casanova, M. (2006) 'The brains of autistic individuals.' *International AWARES OnLine Conference Papers.* Available at www.awares.org/conferences/show_paper.asp?section=000100 010001&conferencecode=000200020012&id=55, accessed on 19 November 2007.

Chapter 5: 'Senseless' and 'Senseful' Ways of Being

1. Taylor, D. (2004) *Think Cat: An Owner's Guide to Feline Psychology.* London: Cassell Illustrated.

2. Grandin, T. (2005) *Animals in Translation: Using the Mysteries of Autism to Decode Animal Behavior.* London: Bloomsbury.

3. Nagel, T. (1974) 'What is it like to be a bat?' *Philosophical Review 83,* 4, 435–50.

4. Griffin, D. (1974) *Listening in the Dark: Acoustic Orientation of Bats and Men.* New York: Dover Publications Inc.

5. Page, G. (1999) *The Singing Gorilla: Understanding Animal Intelligence.* London: Headline Book Publishing.

6. For example, autistic babies have problems in sensory attention and arousal. They orient less to visual information; put objects in their mouths more often; need more cues before they look when someone calls their names; pull away from social touch (Baranek, G. T. (1999) 'Autism during infancy: A retrospective video analysis of sensory–motor and social behaviours at 9–12 months of age.' *Journal of Autism and Developmental Disorders 29,* 213–24); they lack responsiveness to certain sounds, display hypersensitivity to certain foods and insensitivities to pain (Hoshino, Y., Kumashiro, H., Yashima, Y., Tachibana, R., Watanabe, M. and Furukawa, H. (1982) 'Early symptoms of autistic children and its diagnostic significance.' *Folia Psychiatrica*

et Neurologica Japanica 36, 367–74); postures are unusual hand–finger mannerisms and whole body mannerisms (Le Courteur, A., Rutter, M., Lord, C., Rios, P., Robertson, S., Holdgrafer, M. and McLennan, J. (1989) 'Autism diagnostic interview: A standard investigator-based instrument.' *Journal of Autism and Developmental Disorders 19*, 363–87; Lord, C., Rutter, M. and Le Couteur, A. (1994) 'Autism diagnostic interview – revised: A revised version of a diagnostic interview for caregivers of individuals with possible pervasive developmental disorders.' *Journal of Autism and Developmental Disorders 24*, 659–85); when tickled they are easily overexcited and their interest in visual stimuli is atypical (Gillberg, C., Ehlers, S., Schaumann, H., Jacobson, G., Dahlgren, S. O., Lindbolm, R., Bagenhold, A., Tjus, T. and Blinder, E. (1990) 'Autism under age 3 years: A clinical study of 28 cases referred for autistic symptoms in infancy.' *Journal of Child Psychology and Psychiatry 31*, 921–34); and reactions to vestibular tasks are unusual (Gepner, B., Mestre, D., Masson, G. and de Schonen, S. (1995) 'Postural effects of motion vision in young autistic children.' *Neuroreport 6*, 1211–14; Kohen-Raz, R., Volkmar, F. R. and Cohen, D. J. (1992) 'Postural control in children with autism.' *Journal of Autism and Developmental Disorders 22*, 419–32). These and many other autistic 'sensory' symptoms observed during the first year seem to persist into the second year of life (Adrien, J. L., Perrot, A., Sauvage, D., Leddet, I., Larmande, C., Hameury, L. and Barthelemy, C. (1992) 'Early symptoms in autism from family home movies: Evaluation and comparison between 1st and 2nd year of life using I.B.S.E. scale.' *Acta Paedopsychiatrica 55*, 71–75; Adrien, J. L., Lenoir, P., Martineau, J., Perrot, A., Hameury, L., Larmande, C. and Sauvage, D. (1993) 'Blind ratings of early symptoms of autism based upon family home movies.' *Journal of American Academy of Child and Adolescent Psychiatry 32*, 617–26) and that's when a basis for differences in further development is formed. Some researchers suggest relabelling certain disorders that were previously considered 'cognitive' because with recent neuroscientific discoveries the distinction between sensory and cognitive function becomes increasingly unclear (Moore, David (2001) 'Sensory training and special education – can practice make perfect?' *British Journal of Special Education 28*, 3, 138–41).

7. Bogdashina, O. (2003) *Sensory Perceptual Issues in Autism and Asperger Syndrome: Different Sensory Experiences – Different Perceptual Worlds.* London: Jessica Kingsley Publishers.

8. Grandin, T. and Johnson, C. (2005) *Animals in Translation: Using the Mysteries of Autism to Decode Animal Behavior.* London: Bloomsbury.

9. Casanova, M. (2006) 'Brains of the autistic individuals.' *International AWARE On-Line Conference Papers.* Available at www.autism2006.org, accessed on 2 October 2006.

10. Rubenstein, J. L. R. and Merzenich, M. M. (2003, 'Model of autism: increased ratio of excitation/inhibition in key neural systems.' *Genes, Brain and Behavior 2*, 255–67) hypothesise that at least some forms of autism are caused by an increased ratio of excitation/inhibition in sensory, social and emotional systems. Their explanation backs up the 'shower analogy'.

11. Temple Grandin cites animal and human studies (1996, 'My Experiences with Visual Thinking, Sensory Problems and Communication Difficulties.' www.autism.org/temple/visual.html.) that show that restriction of sensory input causes the central nervous system to become overly sensitive to stimulation. Animals placed in an environment that severely restricts sensory input also develop many 'autistic symptoms' such as stereotyped behaviours, hyperactivity and self-injury. The effects of early sensory deprivation are often long-lasting, and the hypersensitivity caused by sensory restriction seems to be relatively permanent. There is a possibility that at least some cases of autism may be a type of deprivation syndrome. Temple Grandin hypothesises that possibly there are secondary central nervous system (CNS) abnormalities which happen as a result of the child's avoidance of input. The initial sensory processing problems with which the child is born cause initial avoidance. However, the limbic system is not mature until the child is about two years old. The possibility of secondary damage to the CNS may account for why young children in early intervention education programmes have better prognosis than children who do not receive special treatment.

12. If it is *visual fragmentation*, the child may see (at the level of sensation) the whole person in front of him. When trying to process what or who is in front of him, the child may see (at the level of interpretation) an eye, or a nose, or a mouth, and then put

all these bits together in his head. That is, autistic children may have no problem visually processing the whole picture; their difficulty may only start when the individual elements must be integrated to form a general idea or understanding at a higher-order conceptual level. For them, the person seems to be bits of a jigsaw puzzle that do not make sense. If it is *auditory fragmentation*, the child may hear (with meaning) 'bits' of sentences surrounded by meaningless blah-blah-blah's, and find it difficult to combine a few words he hears into a meaningful message. Individuals with *proprioceptive* and/or *tactile fragmentation* may perceive their whole body in bits; they may feel an arm, or a shoulder, or a leg, or a nose, but the connections between these parts are not there.

13. Perception by parts requires more time and effort to interpret what is going on with and around them. It may appear as though they do not feel pain, do not listen and do not know what they want. However, they might be processing the sensations, and by the time they get it and understand what these sensations mean, they may be several minutes, or hours, or days, even weeks or months away from the context in which experiences actually happened. For the majority of autistic HSs, the delay may be just a few seconds, but for some, it may well be much longer. For instance, a child may fall down, and not a sound of discomfort, not a wink. When the mother relaxes that the fall was not bad – 'Aaaah!' The toddler *felt* pain a few minutes after the injury. How can outsiders connect the sudden outburst with something that happened ten minutes earlier, for example?

14. Many autistic humans are hypersensitive to fluorescent lights. They can see a 60-cycle flickering, making the room pulsate on and off. Humans with *hyperhearing* are generally very light sleepers; they are frightened by sudden unpredictable sounds (such as, for example, the telephone ringing or baby crying), dislike thunderstorms, crowds, are terrified by haircut, etc. They often cover their ears when the noise is painful for them, though others in the same room may be unaware of any disturbing sounds at all. Sometimes hyperauditory humans make repetitive noises to block out other disturbing sounds. Autistic humans with *olfactory hypersensitivities* cannot tolerate how humans or objects smell, though their carers can be unaware of any smell at all. They run from smells, move away from humans and animals and insist on wearing the same clothes all the time. For some, the

smell or taste of any food is too strong, and they reject it no matter how hungry they are. Some autistic HSs are *hypertactile*; they pull away when humans try to hug them, because they fear being touched. Because of their hypertactility resulting in overwhelming sensations, even the slightest touch can send them to a panic attack. Small scratches that most humans ignore can feel very tormenting to them. Washing the hair turns into an ordeal demanding several humans to complete it. Many individuals refuse to wear certain clothes, as they cannot tolerate the texture on their skin. Some humans with hypertactility overreact to heat or cold, avoid wearing shoes, dislike food of certain textures and avoid getting 'messy'.

15. Humans with *hypovision* may experience trouble figuring out where objects are, as they see just outlines. They may walk around objects, running their hand around the edges so they can recognise what they are. These individuals are attracted to lights and fascinated with reflections and bright-coloured objects. Having entered an unfamiliar room they have to walk around it, touching everything before they settle down. Humans with *hypohearing* may seek sounds, for example enjoying crowds or sirens. They like the noisiest places in the house – kitchens and bathrooms. They often create sounds themselves to stimulate their hearing – banging doors, tapping things, tearing or crumpling paper in the hands, making loud rhythmic noises. Individuals with *hypotaste/hyposmell* chew and smell everything they can get – grass, play dough, toys. They mouth and lick objects, play with faeces, eat mixed food (for instance, sweet and sour). Those with *hypotactility* seem not to feel pain or temperature. They may not notice a wound caused by a sharp object or they seem unaware of a broken bone. They are prone to self-injuries and may bite their hand or bang their head against the wall, just to feel something. Humans with *vestibular hyposensitivity* enjoy and seek all sorts of movement and can spin and swing for a long time without being dizzy. They often rock forth and back or move in circles while rocking the body. Those with *proprioceptive hyposensitivity* have difficulty knowing where their bodies are in space and are often unaware of their body sensations, for example they do not feel hunger.

16. McKean, T. (1994) *Soon Will Come the Light: A View from Inside the Autism Puzzle.* Arlington, TX: Future Horizons.

17. The same is true of other senses if they are hypersensitive: the indirect perception of smell, taste or touch are often defensive strategies to avoid overload and 'keep in touch' with reality. Direct perception in autism is often hyper. It can cause sensory overload resulting in switching to 'mono'.

18. Williams, D. (1996) *Autism: An Inside-Out Approach.* London: Jessica Kingsley Publishers.

19. Kracke, I. (1994) 'Developmental prosopagnosia in Asperger syndrome: Presentation and discussion of an individual case.' *Developmental Medicine and Child Neurology 36,* 873–86.

Chapter 6: Thinking about Thinking

1. Ristau, C. (ed) (1991) *Cognitive Ethology: The Mind of Other Animals.* Hillsdale, NJ: Erlbaum.

2. Koehler, O. (1953) 'Thinking without words.' *Proceedings of the 14th International Zoological Congress,* pp.75–88, Copenhagen.

3. Griffin, D. (1984) *Animal Thinking.* Cambridge, MA: Harvard University Press.

4. Griffin, D. R. (1998) 'From cognition to consciousness.' *Animal Cognition 1,* 1, 3–16.

5. Grandin, T. (1998) 'Consciousness in animals and people with autism.' Available at www.grandin.com/references/animal.consciousness.html, accessed on 19 November 2007.

6. Armstrong-Buck, S. (1989) 'Nonhuman experience: A Whiteheadian analysis.' *Process Studies 18,* 1, 1–18.

7. Gallup, G. Jr (1979) 'Self-recognition in chimpanzees and man: A developmental and comparative perspective.' In M. Lewis and A. Rosenblum (eds) *The Child and Its Family.* New York: Plenum Press.

8. For example, Koko seemed embarrassed when a human noted that she was signing to herself while playing with her dolls and animals toys. Koko was engaged in an imaginative play with her toys, and when finished, she signed 'Good gorilla, good, good'. Koko's teacher was observing the whole performance, and when the gorilla noticed the unwelcome witness's attention she immediately left her dolls. (Patterson, F. (1980) 'Innovative uses

of language by a gorilla: A case study.' In K. Nelson (ed) *Children's Language*. Vol.2. New York: Gardener.)

9. Williams, D. (1996) *Autism: An Inside-Out Approach*. London: Jessica Kingsley Publishers; Williams, D. (2006) *The Jumble Jigsaw: An Insider Approach to the Treatment of Autistic Spectrum 'Fruit Salads'*. London: Jessica Kingsley Publishers.

10. Williams, D. (1998) *Autism and Sensing: The Unlost Instinct*. London: Jessica Kingsley Publishers.

11. Pearce, J. M. (1991). 'The acquisition of abstract and concrete categories by pigeons.' In L. Dachowski and C. Flaherty (eds), *Current Topics in Animal Learning: Brain, Emotion and Cognition*, pp.141–64. New Jersey: Erlbaum.

12. Snyder, A. W. and Barlow, H. (1988) 'Human vision: Revealing the artist's touch.' *Nature 331*, 117–18.

13. Bogdashina, O. (2004) *Communication Issues in Autism and Asperger Syndrome: Do We Speak the Same Language?* London: Jessica Kingsley Publishers.

14. Grandin, T. and Johnson, C. (2005) *Animals in Translation: Using the Mysteries of Autism to Decode Animal Behavior*. London: Bloomsbury.

15. I take the liberty of replacing the original term 'retarded acquisition' with 'delayed acquisition'.

16. Snyder, A. W., Bossomaier, T. and Mitchell, J. D. (2004) 'Concept formation: "Object" attributes dynamically inhibited from conscious awareness.' *Journal of Integrative Neuroscience 3*, 1, 31–46.

17. Snyder, A. W. and Mitchell, J. D. (1999) 'Is integer arithmetic fundamental to mental proceeding? The mind's secret arithmetic.' *Proceedings of the Royal Society of London 266*, 587–92.

18. This hypothesis builds on research that newborns, unlike adults, are probably aware of the raw sensory data available at lower levels of neural processing and that they quite possibly have excellent recall of this information. But with maturation there is a strategy to suppress such awareness. Instead, the mind becomes increasingly aware only of concepts to the exclusion of the details that comprise the concepts. As Snyder puts it, an autistic mind – a mind without paradigms – is more conscious and hence

potentially aware of alternative interpretations. However, there are disadvantages to this 'superability':

- Such a mind would have difficulty in coping with the flood of information and would need routines and structure to make sense of the world, because every detail has to be examined anew each time it is perceived and with equal importance to every other detail.
- There would be lack of (or delay in) development of symbolic systems, such as communication, language and verbal thought (*Ibid.*).

19. Williams, D. (2003) 'Tinted lenses.' *Autism Today Online Magazine.* Available at www.donnawilliams.net/tintedlenses.0.html, accessed on 19 November 2007.

20. Williams, D. (Undated) 'Not thinking in pictures'. Available at www.donnawilliams.net/notthinkinginpics.0.html, accessed on 19 November 2007.

21. O'Neill, J. (1999) *Through the Eyes of Aliens.* London: Jessica Kingsley Publishers.

Chapter 7: What is so Special about Special Abilities?

1. Grandin, T. and Johnson, C. (2005) *Animals in Translation: Using the Mysteries of Autism to Decode Animal Behavior.* London: Bloomsbury.

2. Ransink, A. R. (2004) 'Visual sensing without seeing.' *Psychological Science 15,* 1, 27–32.

3. McCraty, R. (2004) cited in 'Mindsight and precognition.' *JREF Online Newsletter 20,* February 2004. Available at www.randi.org/jr/022004demons.html, accessed on 19 November 2007.

4. Grandin, T. and Johnson, C. (2005) *Animals in Translation: Using the Mysteries of Autism to Decode Animal Behavior.* London: Bloomsbury, p.57.

5. Rupert Sheldrake has collected many well-known facts about animals' ability to *feel* earthquakes, avalanches and other natural disasters well before they actually happen. (Sheldrake, R. (2003) *The Sense of Being Stared At.* London: Hutchinson.)

6. Cited in Cytowic, R. E. (1989) *Synaesthesia: A Union of the Senses.* New York: Springer Verlag.

7. There are several subtypes in each synaesthetic group. Two-sensory synaesthesia may be:

    - coloured-hearing: when a sound triggers the perception of a colour
    - coloured-olfaction: when a smell triggers the perception of a colour
    - coloured-gustation: when a taste triggers the perception of a colour
    - coloured-tactility: when a touch triggers the perception of a colour
    - tactile-hearing: when a sound triggers tactile sensation
    - tactile-vision: when a sight triggers feeling shapes and textures pressing the skin
    - tactile-gustation: when a taste is experienced as a shape
    - audiomotor: when the sounds of different words trigger different postures of the body, and so on.

    Multiple sensory synaesthesia:

    - coloured-numbers: when numbers are heard or read they are experienced as colours
    - coloured-letters: when letters are heard or read they are experienced as colours
    - coloured-graphemes: when words are heard or read they are experienced as colours
    - shaped-numbers: when numbers are heard or read they are experienced as colours.

8. Maurer, D. (1993) 'Neonatal synaesthesia: Implications for the processing of speech and faces.' In B. de Boysson-Bardies, S. de Schonen, P. Jusczyk, P. McNeilage and J. Morton (eds) *Developmental Neurocognition: Speech and Face Processing in the First Year of Life.* Dordrecht: Kluwer Academic Publishers.

9. Dehay, C., Bullier, J. and Kennedy, H. (1984) 'Transient projections from the fronto-parietal and temporal cortex to areas 17, 18, and 19 in the kitten.' *Experimental Brain Research 57*, 208–12.

10. Baron-Cohen, S., Harrison, J., Golstein, L. and Wyke, M. (1993) 'Coloured speech perception: Is synaesthesia what happens when modularity breaks down?' *Perception 22*, 419–26.

11. Bogdashina, O. (2004) *Communication Issues in Autism and Asperger Syndrome: Do We Speak the Same Language?* London: Jessica Kingsley Publishers.

12. Page, G. (1999) *The Singing Gorilla: Understanding Animal Intelligence.* London: Headline Book Publishing. This summarises this argument very well: 'A given animal's highest intelligence will be demonstrated in its natural habitat, where it needs this intelligence. Some animals do much better on certain tests in their natural environment than on the same tests in the laboratory.'

13. Grandin, T. and Johnson, C. (2005) *Animals in Translation: Using the Mysteries of Autism to Decode Animal Behavior.* London: Bloomsbury, p.62.

Chapter 8: Language and Communication: Let's Talk about Talking

1. Bogdashina, O. (2004) *Communication Issues in Autism and Asperger Syndrome: Do We Speak the Same Language?* London: Jessica Kingsley Publishers.

2. The answer is not provided. If you are not interested, just skip it.

3. Bogdashina, O. (2005) *Theory of Mind and the Triad of Perspectives on Autism and Asperger Syndrome: A View from the Bridge.* London: Jessica Kingsley Publishers.

4. Williams, D. (1998) *Autism and Sensing.* London: Jessica Kingsley Publishers.

5. Prizant, B. M. (1982) 'Gestalt processing and Gestalt language acquisition in autism.' *Topics in Language Disorders 3*, 16–23; Prizant, B. M. (1983) 'Echolalia in autism: Assessment and intervention.' *Seminar in Speech and Language 4*, 63–78; Bogdashina, O. (2004) *Communication Issues in Autism and Asperger Syndrome: Do We Speak the Same Language?* London: Jessica Kingsley Publishers.

Chapter 9: Emotions: Love Me? Love Me Not?

1. Shweder, R. A. (1994) '"You're not sick, you're just in love": Emotion as an interpretive system.' In P. Ekman and R. J.

Davidson (eds) *The Nature of Emotion: Fundamental Questions.* New York: Oxford University Press, pp.32–44.

2. As Shweder [*Ibid.*] puts it, emotions represent somatic and affective experience not simply as a feeling (such as tiredness or tension or a heartache or feeling sick) but as a perception (for example, being in love, or betrayal by trusted friends) and a plan (withdrawal, retaliation, etc.). Both parts are equally important. Damasio shows how physical manifestation of fear, for example, such as accelerated heart beat, actually contributes to the feeling of fear rather than being a mere by-product (Damasio, A. (2000) *The Feeling of What Happens: Body, Emotion and the Meaning of Consciousness.* London: William Heinemann.)

3. Carter, R. (1998) *Mapping the Mind.* London: Weidenfield & Nicolson.

4. Grandin, T. and Johnson, C. (2005) *Animals in Translation: Using the Mysteries of Autism to Decode Animal Behavior.* London: Bloomsbury.

5. The elephant orphanage in Nairobi National Park, The David Sheldrick Wildlife Trust. Available at www.sheldrickwildlifetrust.org, accessed on 19 November 2007.

6. Panksepp, J. (1994) 'The basics of basic emotions.' In P. Ekman and R. J. Davidson *The Nature of Emotion: Fundamental Questions.* New York: Oxford University Press, pp.20–24.

7. Crepeau, L. and Panksepp, J. (1988) 'Dual olfactory system and cat smell-attenuated juvenile rat play.' *Neuroscience Abstracts 14,* 1104.

8. However, the ability to identify and 'name' what one is feeling is a different matter altogether. The activity of labelling is arbitrary; it is independent of the emotional experience. The choice of words to describe the emotion often depends on communicators' intentions. For example, some words appear to emphasise the physiological reaction component ('aroused' or 'tired'); some are quite cognitive (for example, 'bewildered' or 'curious'). Others focus on somewhat specific sociomotivation (for instance, 'jealous'). Still others highlight the action tendency (like 'hostile') (Scherer, K. R. 'Toward a concept of "modal emotions".' In P. Ekman and R. J. Davidson (eds) *The Nature of Emotion: Fundamental Questions.* New York: Oxford University Press, pp.25–31.)

9. Ekman, P. (1994) 'All emotions are basic.' In P. Ekman and R. J. Davidson (eds) *The Nature of Emotion: Fundamental Questions.* New York: Oxford University Press, pp.15–19.

10. Kanner, L. (1943) 'Autistic disturbances of affective contact.' *Nervous Child 2*, 217–50, see p.242.

11. Ricks, D. and Wing, L. (1975) 'Language, communication and the use of symbols in normal and autistic children.' *Journal of Autism and Childhood Schizophrenia 5*, 191–221.

12. Sinclair, J. (1992) 'Bridging the gaps: An inside-out view of autism.' In E. Schopler and G. B. Mesibov (eds) *High-Functioning Individuals with Autism.* New York: Plenum Press.

13. Sinclair, J. (1989) *Some Thoughts about Empathy.* Available at http://web.syr.edu/%7Ejisincla/empathy.htm, accessed on 19 November 2007.

14. Schneider, E. (1999) *Discovering My Autism: Apologia Pro Vita Sua (with apologies to Cardinal Newman).* London: Jessica Kingsley Publishers.

15. Williams, D. (1994) *Somebody Somewhere.* London: Doubleday.

16. Cited in Goleman, D. (1995) *Emotional Intelligence.* London: Bloomsbury.

17. O'Neill, J. (1999) *Through the Eyes of Aliens: A Book about Autistic People.* London: Jessica Kingsley Publishers.

18. Grandin, T. (1992) 'Autistic emotions.' *The Advocate*, Spring 1992, pp.6–8.

Chapter 10: Challenging Behaviours: Who Challenges Whom?

1. O'Neill, J. (1999) *Through the Eyes of Aliens: A Book about Autistic People.* London: Jessica Kingsley Publishers.

2. Grandin, T. (1996) *Thinking in Pictures and Other Reports from My Life with Autism.* New York: Vintage Books.

3. Bogdashina, O. (2003) *Sensory Perceptual Issues in Autism and Asperger Syndrome: Different Sensory Experiences – Different Perceptual Worlds.* London: Jessica Kingsley Publishers.

4. Delacato, C. (1974) *The Ultimate Stranger: The Autistic Child.* Novato, CA: Academic Therapy Publications.

5. Grandin, T. and Johnson, C. (2005) *Animals in Translation: Using the Mysteries of Autism to Decode Animal Behavior.* London: Bloomsbury.

6. Lawson, W. (2001) *Understanding and Working with the Spectrum of Autism: An Insider's View.* London: Jessica Kingsley Publishers.

7. Williams, D. (1996) *Autism: An Inside-Out Approach.* London: Jessica Kingsley Publishers.

Dasha's Library: Selected Bibliography

About autism

Blackman, L. (1999) *Lucy's Story: Autism and other Adventures.* London: Jessica Kingsley Publishers.

Bogdashina, O. (2003) *Sensory Perceptual Issues in Autism and Asperger Syndrome: Different Sensory Experiences – Different Perceptual Worlds.* London: Jessica Kingsley Publishers.

Bogdashina, O. (2004) *Communication Issues in Autism and Asperger Syndrome: Do We Speak the Same Language?* London: Jessica Kingsley Publishers.

Bogdashina, O. (2005) *Theory of Mind and the Triad of Perspectives on Autism and Asperger Syndrome: A View from the Bridge.* London: Jessica Kingsley Publishers.

Casanova, M. (2006) 'The brains of autistic individuals.' *International OnLine AWARES Conference Papers.* Available at www.awares.org/conferences/show_paper.asp?section=000100 010001&conferencecode=000200020012&id=55, accessed on 19 November 2007.

Delacato, C. (1974) *The Ultimate Stranger: The Autistic Child.* Novato, CA: Academic Therapy Publications.

Grandin, T. (1996) *Thinking in Pictures and Other Reports from My Life with Autism.* New York: Vintage Books.

Grandin, T. and Johnson, C. (2005) *Animals in Translation: Using the Mysteries of Autism to Decode Animal Behavior.* London: Bloomsbury.

Kanner, L. (1943) 'Autistic disturbances of affective contact.' *Nervous Child 2,* 217–50.

Lawson, W. (2001) *Understanding and Working with the Spectrum of Autism: An Insider's View.* London: Jessica Kingsley Publishers.

O'Neill, J. (1999) *Through the Eyes of Aliens: A Book about Autistic People.* London: Jessica Kingsley Publishers.

Prince-Hughes, D. (2004) *Songs of the Gorilla Nation: My Journey through Autism.* New York: Three Rivers Press.

Sinclair, J. (1992) 'Bridging the gaps: An inside-out view of autism.' In E. Schopler and G. B. Mesibov (eds) *High-Functioning Individuals with Autism.* New York: Plenum Press.

Sinclair, J. (1993) 'Don't mourn for us.' *Our Voice 3.* Syracuse, NY: Autism Network International.

Snyder, A. W. (1998) 'Breaking mindset.' *Mind Language 13*, 1–10.

Snyder, A. W., Bossomaier, T. and Mitchell, J. D. (2004) 'Concept formation: "Object" attributes dynamically inhibited from conscious awareness.' *Journal of Integrative Neuroscience 3*, 1, 31–46.

Williams, D. (1996) *Autism: An Inside-Out Approach.* London: Jessica Kingsley Publishers.

Williams, D. (1998) *Autism and Sensing: The Unlost Instinct.* London: Jessica Kingsley Publishers.

Williams, D. (2003) *Exposure Anxiety – The Invisible Cage: An Exploration of Self-Protection Responses in the Autism Spectrum and Beyond.* London: Jessica Kingsley Publishers.

Williams, D. (2006) *The Jumbled Jigsaw: An Insider's Approach to the Treatment of Autistic Spectrum 'Fruit Salads'.* London: Jessica Kingsley Publishers.

About cats

Bessant, C. (2002) *What Cats Want.* London: Metro.

Haddon, C. (2003) *How to Read Your Cat's Mind.* London: Little Books.

Halls, V. (2004) *Cat Confidential.* London: Bantam Press.

Heath, S. (2000) *Why Does My Cat…?* London: Souvenir Press.

Taylor, D. (2004) *Think Cat: An Owner's Guide to Feline Psychology.* London: Cassell Illustrated.